RON PIGRAM

Discovering Walks in Hertfordshire

SHIRE PUBLICATIONS LTD

Contents

The maps were drawn by D. R. Darton. The cover photograph, of Ashwell, is by Cadbury Lamb.

British Library Cataloguing in Publication data available.

 First edition published 1973. This second edition, including completely new walks, published 1985. Number 170 in the Discovering series. ISBN 0 85263 742 X.

Set in 9 point Times roman and printed in Great Britain by C. I. Thomas & Sons (Haverfordwest) Ltd, Press Buildings, Merlins Bridge, Haverfordwest, Dyfed.

Introduction

This book is a guide to discovering the Hertfordshire countryside on foot. There are fifteen walks, each revealing a different type of countryside, so that if you do them all you will be surprised at the range of types of scenery in the county.

The first edition of *Discovering Walks in Hertfordshire,* was published in 1973. But the countryside is always changing, and so this book is not just a revision of the walks previously published, but a compilation of brand-new rambles for everyone to enjoy.

The fifteen walks in this book were all trodden during the few months before the book was published. They include two or three quite short walks to encourage those readers who might feel a little out of practice to come along and enjoy the open air.

All the walks are circular, especially designed for those using their cars, but care has been taken to include walks which can be made from convenient railway stations or bus routes. Farmers often complain that gates and openings are not refastened after a wayfarer has passed; most experienced walkers are careful to do this to prevent cattle and sheep from straying.

It is advisable to carry with you the Ordnance Survey map for the area; Hertfordshire is broadly contained on sheets 165, 166 and 167 of the 1:50,000 (Landranger) series, where paths are marked (usually) in red. Larger-scale (1:25,000) Pathfinder maps are also available. Do not altogether trust symbols and signs that you see on a map whilst planning your walk. The fastest vanishing 'clue' is the wood. Some are felled almost overnight, and a wood is mentioned in these pages which is not depicted on the Ordnance Survey map. However, woods and buildings marked on the map are usually the clues that will set you off again on the right path should you experience any difficulty out in the fields.

Every care has been taken to see that the paths are open to the public, although there can be no guarantee that rights of way still exist. Parking for cars can usually be found at the start of the walk, but in towns you will find nearby car parks.

Much work has been done by organised groups employed by the county council and other bodies, resulting in the repair of fallen bridges over streams, stiles and other field furniture. The author has found this a very refreshing experience during the planning and surveying of the walks in this book, as such work, together with some helpful waymarking by coloured posts at strategic points, has resulted in many trouble-free and enjoyable days out. Remember to be well shod and expect some mud, even in the summer. Please leave the wild flowers, especially during bluebell time, for others to enjoy.

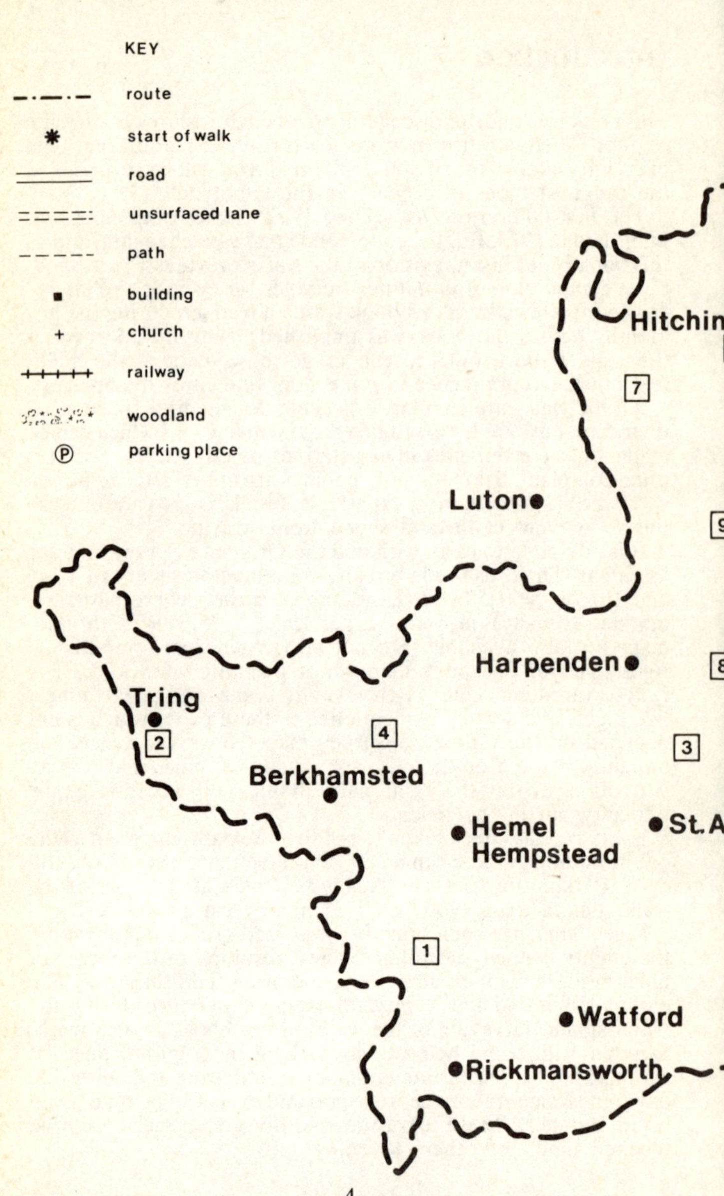
KEY
route
start of walk
road
unsurfaced lane
path
building
church
railway
woodland
parking place
Hitchin
7
Luton
9
Harpenden
8
Tring
2
4
3
Berkhamsted
Hemel
Hempstead
St. A
1
Watford
Rickmansworth

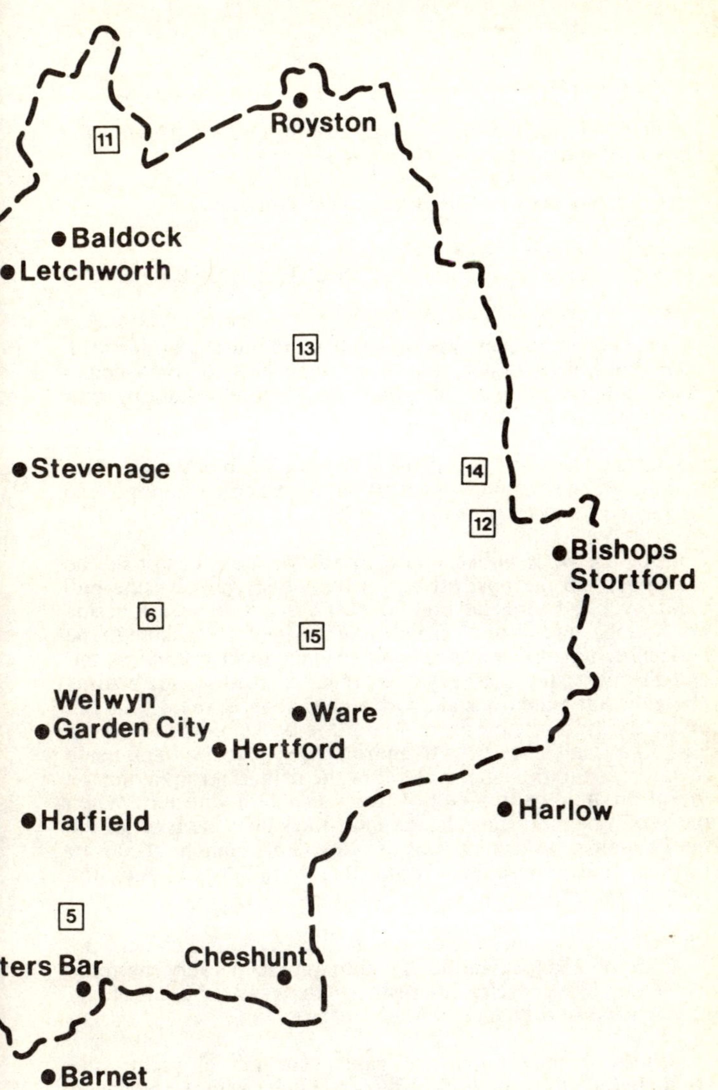
Royston
11
Baldock
Letchworth
13
Stevenage
14
12
Bishops Stortford
6
15
Welwyn Garden City
Ware
Hertford
Harlow
Hatfield
5
ters Bar
Cheshunt
Barnet

1. Sarratt

Circular walk from Sarratt by way of Church End, Mountwood Farm, Chenies and Sarratt Bottom.

Start: Sarratt Green, the Boot public house.
Grid reference: TQ 043993.
Distance: 4¼ miles (6.8 km).
Ordnance Survey maps: 1:50,000 sheet 176; 1:25,000 sheet TQ 09.

This easy-going Chilterns walk starts and finishes in Hertfordshire, but you cross the sparkling river Chess to visit Chenies Place and church, in Buckinghamshire, before wandering near the riverbank for the return.

Sarratt is an easy-to-find village near Watford. It possesses a fine wide green with ample parking, and some convenient pubs to quench your thirst.

From the Boot public house by the village green cross the greensward to the post office, on the left if you have the pub behind you. 30 yards beyond the post office, find a track beside Ivy Cottage, and go on to cross a stile in a field. Keep close to the hedgeline (left) to an iron stile at a wide grassy track. Cross this and the next stile before you to reach a small wood, bearing along the left-hand track at a fork almost at once, so that you run under the trees, with rails and later the backs of houses on the left. At a small lane, cross to an iron cage-wicket on the far side (a yard or so to the left), and follow the path as it runs along the top of the field, with a belt of trees at first on your left. When they end, the path runs ahead, and strikes over the brow of the field towards the distant roof of Holy Cross church, at Sarratt Church End. There is a swing-gate to allow you into the churchyard.

Church End was once the centre of old Sarratt. The church, the Cock inn and the handful of buildings remain a very charming picture. The church is interesting with its saddleback roof and the nave and chancel forming a cross.

Return to the churchyard gate, your arrival point, and continue on, along the *lower* side of the field, with the hedge on your left. Soon you will reach a gate on the left, where the path passes through to reach an avenue of trees. Take the path that crosses the avenue and which runs directly downhill, keeping the hedgeline on your left.

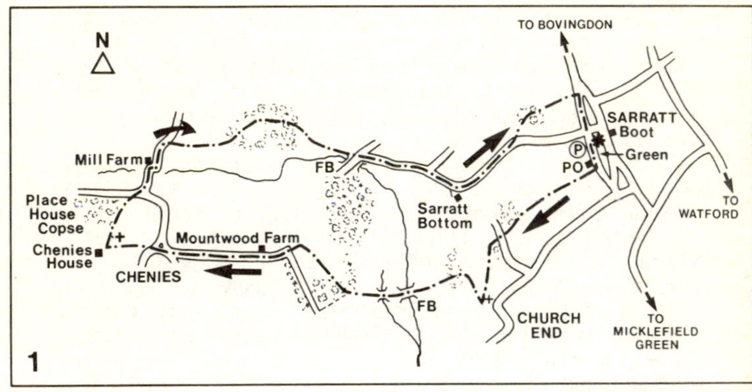

The valley below is reached by way of the stile ahead and then the short enclosed path. Near the bottom, as the path turns sharply to the right, go *left* over the stile here into the meadow on your left, then go at once right to the pretty little wooden footbridge which crosses the river Chess.

The grassy path from the footbridge leads forward (crossing another footbridge on the way) to the side of the wood ahead. Cross the stile into the wood, and look for another stile, on the right, after only 20 yards. This marks the official footpath, which runs from here half-left, uphill, across the field (at first near a projecting angle of the trees on the left) to the hedgeline on the far side, turning left to keep the hedge on its right to a wide field track at the top. (However, if the field is in deep crop during early summer you may find it convenient to continue along the path reached upon first entering the wood, turning right to make your way around this field by the upper track.)

Follow this track round for another 250 yards, when the buildings of Mountwood Farm appear. Go through the concrete yard, keeping the buildings on the right, and on by the straight little farm lane all the way to a road at Chenies. Cross directly to the green, keeping the pump on the left, and go on by a fine gravel drive to the church and manor house.

Chenies church is important for its special chapel to the Russells, the family of the Dukes of Bedford, whose elaborate tombs can be glimpsed if you are fortunate enough to find the church open. There is also much to see in Chenies House, which is occasionally open to the public.

From the manor house gates there is a good path on the right.

Take this; it runs past the side of the church and downhill towards a small wood (Place House Copse). As you go, there are pleasant little views across the Chess valley on the right-hand side. Enter the wood at the stile, but keep to the right-hand path that runs directly downhill to a road at the bottom. Be careful here; there is a sharp bend!

Cross the road to take the little lane opposite, which still brings you downhill. Pass an over-restored millhouse and cross the bridge, also passing the white-painted Mill Farm (on your left). Walk along the lane for 200 yards beyond the farm, then go into the field on the right through a gap (signposted).

Go straight forward across the meadow (there may be a strand of wire to guide you on your right) towards the projecting spur of woodland on the far side. The river Chess runs parallel to your course, far away on the right. Cross the stile at this narrow woodland spur and keep to the left side of the next meadow to another stile in the far corner, leading into a large wood. Once again, keep straight ahead by the path, and on the far side bear away slightly right with it so that you are closer to the riverbank. The path now runs on, with the river not far away on the right, over stiles to a concrete trackway at a bend (a few yards to the right is another footbridge over the Chess).

The walk goes forward by the concrete track with the river (and watercress beds) on the right. Ignore the first turn on the left, and continue along the river lane for another 200 yards or so to a second lane on the left, with a white cottage on the corner (Cakebread Cottage). This is Sarratt Bottom.

Turn left up the lane as it climbs quite steeply out of the valley. Almost at the top, just after passing an entrance on the right, leave the lane at a footpath sign marking the start of a path running into the wood on the left. This gradually leaves the lane and runs slightly leftwards between the trees. In another 100 yards or so you strike a small trackway in the wood, which leads leftwards for a few yards to reveal a stile at the wood corner. Cross this, and keep along the side of the field ahead, with the hedge and wooden rails on your right. At the end you will reach an enclosed track, which soon brings you out at the far end of Sarratt Green. Now turn right to your starting point.

2. Tring

Circular walk from Tring by way of Tring Park, Grim's Ditch, Buckland Wood and Hastoe.

Start: Tring High Street, by the parish church.
Grid reference: SU 923113.
Distance: 7 miles (11.3 km).
Ordnance Survey maps: 1:50,000 sheet 165; 1:25,000 sheet SU 90/91.

The hills above Tring were loved and walked by the poet Rupert Brooke during the early years of the twentieth century. Much of this woodland country remains for us to enjoy. From these rolling Chiltern Hills there are some remarkable panoramas over the west Hertfordshire countryside.

The walk starts from Tring High Street, at Tring parish church. Walk westwards (to the left, if you are facing the church) to Akeman Street, the first turning on the left. At the end of the street turn left after passing the front of Tring Zoological Museum (which is open, free, to the public every day except Christmas, Good Friday, New Year's Day and May Day).

The little 'no through road' passes the side of the building; now take a little tarmac path on the right, 200 yards from the junction and beside a timbered, gabled lodge. This is the footpath to Tring Park. It runs up to cross the bypass, opened in 1975, by a graceful spiral footbridge. At the top, take a look into the parkland and note the clear path leading from the iron swing-gate at the bridge and running half-left towards the distant woods.

By this undulating path you reach the woods at a gate. Carry on uphill by a wide drive through the woods that leads straight to a stone obelisk (Nell Gwynn's Column). Continue straight on uphill, ignoring a right-hand drive, and another 200 yards will bring you to another landscape feature — a stone Doric portico with columns, which is purely a facade. At this landmark go squarely right with the drive for about the same distance to reach a drive junction with a drive on the left, some cleared areas of woodland and, at the time of survey, a helpful footpath signpost. Here go left along the drive, with the cleared area now on your right, until you reach an iron gate and a wooden side-gate at Fox Cottages. Go through the gate, but at once turn right over a stile, following a 'Ridgeway' footpath sign. The path now runs along the side of the woodland, skirting the back gardens of houses. It later crosses a drive and winds right and left as a border path to reach a stile in open grassland. Here cross, and go leftwards along the side of the field to another stile at a wide flint-lined lane.

Now turn right along the wide country way, which runs quite straight on the high ground to pass Wick Farm and later a house. There are some good views, too, as you drop down to a cross junction at Marlins Hill, the normal metalled lane.

At the lane go leftwards for 250 yards towards the large wooded area on the right side. At the wood you will find a stile and sign (right), a few yards beyond the wide shallow depression, marking Grim's Ditch, which forms the boundary line of the wood.

Cross the stile into the wood, but take the right-hand path that runs just inside the wood, with Grim's Ditch just to your right. (The ancient earthwork can be seen also at other Chiltern woodlands in the area.) Trace out this border path that runs ahead and, upon reaching the open fields again at a point where the main wood turns away to the left, continue straight ahead over to the gap opposite, to reach and cross the track coming up from High Scrubs Wood towards Hastoe.

Carry on in the same direction, now guided by a hedgeline which should be on your right hand, with the farm buildings of Longcroft ahead. Later, you find the field edge runs out to the left for some 100 yards: then the official path runs over to the corner of the small wood ahead and thence through the trees to reach a lane just on the right, but it is easy to skirt around the field with the fencing on your right to reach the lane just before you at a gate.

On reaching the lane go right and then turn left along a rough trackway on the left, opposite Longcroft buildings. The lane should be marked 'Master Breed', referring to the farm along the way. The track takes you out of Hertfordshire, and the pole-lined way also marks a district boundary; you pass some cottages and descend to pass the farm buildings away on your left.

Pass the white gates around the farm and carry on along the lane as it climbs the slight rise on the far side. *At this point, some 400 yards after leaving the Longcroft lane, you may either carry on by the lane to Leylands Farm and rejoin the walk at the end of this paragraph, or follow the main route, which leaves the lane as soon as you reach the top of the rise.* Look for a rather dilapidated white swing-gate on the left, beside wire fencing that separates the farm 'dumps' from the field. Turn off the lane at the gate, following the fencing on the left hand, to a corner of the wood ahead; cross the bars of the wooden rails into the wood, and follow the thin path ahead for some 100 yards before bearing gently right with it to walk just inside the wood as open fields appear on your right. The border path continues near the side of

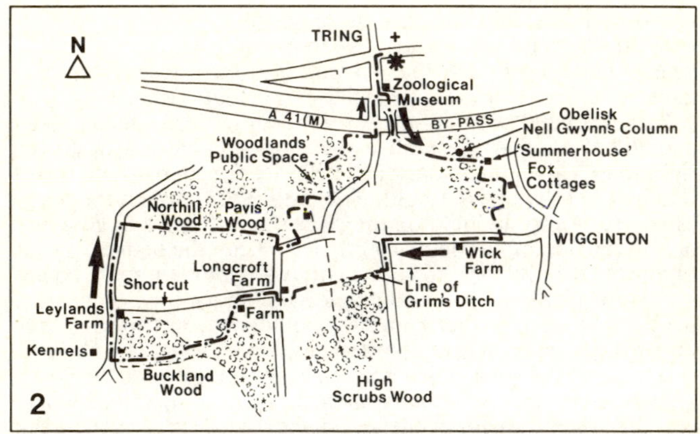

the wood for another 200 yards or so, but when the line of the wood again swings away sharply on the right, keep *straight ahead*, in the direction which you have taken for some time, for a further 200 yards to reach the other side of the wood, with open country this time on your left. You may see a stile leading out of the wood now, but ignore it and continue along the side of the wood, beneath the trees, by a good clear cart track that runs ahead, with open land on your left, all the way to a lane at a remote lane junction. Now go right uphill along the lane, with the trees of Buckland Wood, through which you have just passed, on the right (on a hot day it is pleasant to trace your own path through the border trees). The lane passes kennels and continues to climb gently to pass Leylands Farm on the right.

After Leylands Farm (where short-distance walkers rejoin), continue along the lane uphill to the top, where you are some 800 feet (240 m) above sea level, in very rural country. On reaching the line of trees at the summit, take the wide track on the right, which is well marked with a board, into Northill Wood. (The track will be seen just after passing a concrete entrance and a pylon on the right.) Now comes a grand walk through the wood which lines the top of the hills: keep at once to the right-hand path that generally hugs the right side of the wood. In three quarters of a mile you will reach the far end of the wood (here marked with a board as 'Pavis Wood') at wooden posts, with a gravel path just beyond. Turn right for the few yards along the path to a tiny lane at a bend; turn left here and follow it gently downhill for no more than 150 yards to a stile beside an iron gate on the left. A footpath sign is opposite.

Cross the stile into a field, keeping close to the right side, where the hedge is interspersed with four larch trees. Here you have a surprise view of the valleys west of Tring.

Pass through the gap at the far right corner into a second field and still keep near the right hedge: it winds out a little to the right to reveal another wide gap in 50 yards or so, marked by two fine holly bushes on the right. The path runs between them and as you turn into the field on the right you will see a large house on the far side of the field, slightly left. Keep the hedge on your right until it turns away to your right, when another house comes into view. Continue across the field, aiming for the iron gate on the far side, roughly between the two houses (only the gap may be obvious, as the gate is often left open).

At the gravel track which is reached, go left towards the house known as Hastoe Grove. As you reach the front, marked with an upright stone, look for a stile and sign on your right, as the track turns to run to the right of the house. There is a sign in the woodland, too, stating that it is the Woodlands Public Open Space. Here cross the stile on your right into the wood and follow the path that runs with boundary fencing just to the right. The path follows the side of the wood, running just inside the treeline, for 150 yards until a gate appears ahead at a small lane.

Do not go up to the gate, however, but turn sharp left some yards before it, so that you follow the clear woodland path that runs from it. The path runs clearly on, with the fencing marking the lane away on your right only very *occasionally* seen. Ignore any tiny wayside paths on the left and keep to the main path as it reaches a cross track in the woods (wooden post right) after 200 yards or so. Here, as you continue straight over and on by your path, the ground starts to fall more steeply, and you will meet another path in 50 yards that traces the higher ground of the steep downhill contours of the wood. Go right along this path, with the ground falling steeply to your left, giving light and glimpses of the lower farmland west of Tring. (You may soon hear the noise of traffic using the Tring bypass.) This new path continues to move gently downwards through the trees for a further 100 yards or so, then turns leftwards to run more steeply downhill, becoming wider as you come down to the bottom of the wood, meeting a cross track that runs along the foot of the slope, with the bypass fencing and bushes just ahead. Here go right along the bottom path; you will quickly be out in open country, following the bypass fencing, and with some good views of the town of Tring away on your left. The path runs down to a lane at a bridge carrying the bypass road. Now go left under the bridge and at the next junction go right then left (past the museum again) along Akeman Street to the town centre.

3. Sandridge

Circular walk from Sandridge, by way of Nomansland and Ayres End, or shortened via Pismire Spring.

Start: Sandridge church.
Grid reference: TL 170105.
Distance: 6½ miles (10.5 km) or 5½ miles (8.9 km).
Ordnance Survey maps: 1:50,000 sheet 166; 1:25,000 sheet TL 11.

Walkers used to the ridges and 'bottoms' of the Chilterns will find this walk a stimulating and different experience. This is open country, with wide views from the high ground above the river Ver.

The walk starts from a gravelled track on the far side of the Lyndon Eventide Home, a Salvation Army house that stands beside Sandridge church on the Wheathampstead to St Albans road.

This signposted track (which can also be reached from the path crossing the churchyard) runs past the backs of houses at first, to reach Langley Grove, an estate road nearby. From the iron gate opposite, strike ahead by a clear field track which, after 300 yards, reaches a screen of trees. Then, after hugging the right-hand hedge for another 250 yards or so, the path moves inside the wood, running between the trees of its left side, before it breaks out into a field. With the hedge on your left, continue to a metal and wooden gate that stands beside a wooden stile at Hammonds Lane. Turn right along this tiny backwater towards Hammonds Farm, the buildings on the left at the top of the rise.

Turn left up the farm approach and go between the brick gateways, with the cottage on your right, to enter the yard. Go through and follow a track which veers left to continue along the left side of fields, after a while following a well clipped hedge. Cross directly over another tiny lane, and keep on by the path as it passes the side of three fields, then bends right. (The buildings of Nomansland Farm may be seen on the left as you pass through the first field.) The path, with the hedge now on the right, runs on to an iron gate. Beyond, the path leads on with the scrub of Nomansland Common on either side; keep forward to the crossroads ahead.

Nomansland Common is popular for picnics, games and model aircraft. Its name comes from the wrangling which occurred between the Abbots of St Albans and those of Westminster,

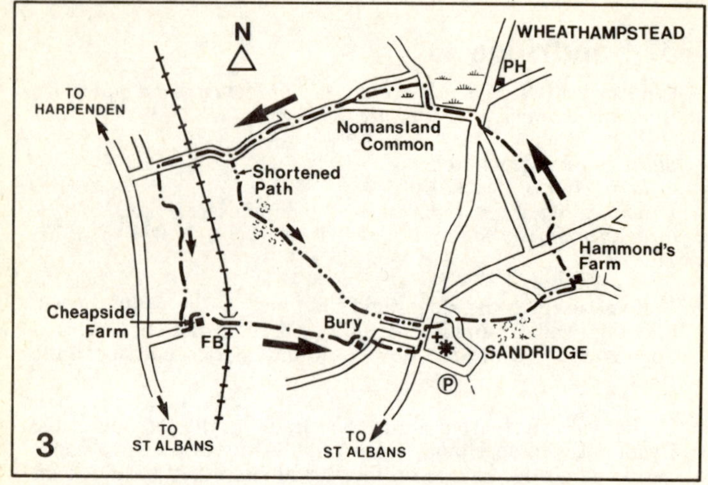

who ruled over the nearby village of Wheathampstead. Here was fought the second battle of St Albans in 1461. Hertfordshire levies met here before proceeding to Tilbury in 1588, and Montgomery met his troops here in 1944. The common was the scene of early nineteenth-century bare-fist fights.

Follow the valley road signposted to Harpenden and Redbourn, by keeping along the wide grassy verge for a quarter of a mile, then turn up Down Green Lane, on the right. Go uphill for 300 yards, past old gravel workings, then take the clear track on the left marked by concrete bollards. It is a charming wooded path through the upper part of the common and runs directly forward for over 800 yards. When you reach a lane on the western side of the common, go right along it, soon passing West End Farm. The road runs uphill to reach a wide green; here take the left-hand fork and carry on by the lane, soon fringed by some fine trees, to pass Ayres End House (right).

From this point note the start of tracks on the left side of the road. You will pass one on the left after 500 yards, near a bend in the lane (with the railway line and trains perhaps to be glimpsed in the distance from the opening). This track will allow you to take the short return path to Sandridge *(for instructions to shorten the walk from here, see the end of the main description)*.

The main walk continues along the lane to cross the railway bridge within 200 yards. Keep on, but after passing a large house on the right, named By-ways, and *before* reaching a lane on the right (which is 500 yards from the bridge) leave the lane for a clear hedgeside path on the left starting from a field-gate/stile (signposted). The path should be quite clear and follows the hedge and a broad band of trees on the right so that you leave the lane far behind you, and have fine open views on the left hand. At the end of the field the hedge and path make a left turn before bending right, again to continue over gently falling ground into a shallow valley. There are some fine hedgerow trees on your right as you go. The path turns right, passing through a hedge at the lower field corner into a wide field rising out of the valley. Follow the path for 100 yards, then, on reaching the opening from a field on the right, turn squarely leftwards to follow a farm track as it runs uphill. The helpful line of bushes that once marked the line of the footpath has gone, but you should have no difficulty keeping with the track to run up to a good asphalt farm track on higher ground in a quarter of a mile or so.

Turn left on this track towards the buildings of Cheapside Farm. At the black barns bear left, passing the main farm buildings on your right to go over the field-gate at the end into the field on the right. Cross the grass towards the far hedge (which shields the line of the railway, here in cutting) and keep the farmhouse and its buildings behind you. At the hedge you should have no trouble finding the footbridge which carries the footpath over the railway. From here a firm path runs ahead and in about half a mile turns leftwards to skirt the boundary line of Sandridgebury (a large house) to reach the lane ahead at a stile. Cross to the stile almost opposite, with the village of Sandridge just ahead, and follow the path as it moves gradually leftwards to pick up and follow the line of a hedge before reaching a recreation ground and, quickly, the village street again. The church is just to your left.

Shortened return to Sandridge. From the lane, just before the railway, go left at the track described and follow a hedge on the left downhill. Keep to the firm path as it climbs beside the trees of Pismire Spring and on to touch the end of Well Wood before it strides quite clearly across a ridge, 400 feet up. There are some fine views from this part of the walk, far over towards Nomansland. Continue gently downhill towards the village, where the track meets the road, to complete the walk.

4. Great Gaddesden

Circular walk from Great Gaddesden by way of Gaddesden Place, St Margaret's and Nettleden.

Start: Great Gaddesden, Cock and Bottle inn.
Grid reference: TL 030112.
Distance: 3¾ miles (6.0 km)
Ordnance Survey maps: 1:50,000 sheet.166; 1:25,000 sheet TL 01.

This is a short walk around the hamlet of Great Gaddesden, deep in the Chilterns. It is undemanding, a ramble for all seasons, but especially beautiful in the spring, when the yellow bloom of the oilseed rape and the drifts of bluebells in the surrounding woods make a brave parade of colour.

Great Gaddesden straggles up the hill on the west side of the Gade valley, just out of sight of the Hemel Hempstead sprawl. This part of Hertfordshire is composed of undulations overlooking the river. Gaddesden, in spite of a row of modern housing, is still the essential hamlet of the inn (the Cock and Bottle), the church and some grand old cottages that have a secure grip on the hillside. There is plenty of car parking near the inn; do not attempt to park along the narrow and busy valley road.

First take the footpath opposite the Cock and Bottle inn, following it past a bungalow and on beside a hedge, with the river winding below. At a stile at a hedge corner, cross and go downhill over grass, bearing a little right at the lower ground to pass over the river by the little wooden footbridge. Continue up to reach a stile set between the brick walls of the farm buildings on the main road.

From the stile opposite a footpath runs uphill towards Gaddesden Place, the large mansion on the hill. Reach the path by crossing the first stile, then the second stile immediately on the right beside the cottage. The path runs up past the front of the cottage before you. At the end, set a course towards an upper stile that may be seen, set in wire, well to the left of a clump of trees about halfway up the hill, and left also of the mansion. Cross this stile and another just ahead (you can recover your breath while admiring the very fine views that you have over the valley from this height). Continue in the same approximate direction set by your passage through the stiles, taking you gradually further away from the house as you climb to the upper pasture. With the house now well to the right, you will

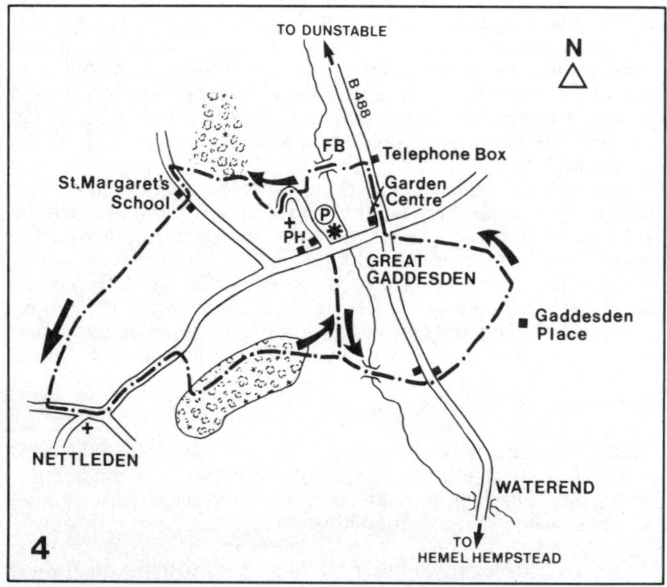

find another stile set in the wire fencing of the top field, some distance left of the field's iron gate.

Gaddesden Place. This mansion, set so imposingly upon a ridge, was built by James Wyatt in 1768 upon classical lines. On a bleak night in 1905 the whole of the central core of the building went up in flames. The conflagration was so brisk that there was little that the primitive firefighters of the district could do. The house was later rebuilt.

Upon reaching the stile, cross and pass through into a field that starts to slope downhill again, with the rooftops of Great Gaddesden away in the distance. Keep beside the wire (left) that marks the edge of the field, and at the lower corner pass through a 'pinch' into the large lower field. Here turn squarely left to cross directly towards the road junction that you can see far below (the red roof of a garden centre provides an easy landmark). At the bottom cross a gate to the main road again, at crossroads.

Now turn right along the main road for 250 yards until you reach a green-painted telephone box near the Parish Hall, on the right. Take the signposted footpath directly opposite the box;

the path quickly leads over a water-meadow to the stream again, which is crossed by a ramshackle wooden footbridge. Upon gaining the far side, swing leftwards and go through the field gap towards the houses. Cross a stile ahead to get into the street and go *uphill* along the housing road, turning left towards garages at the top. Beyond the garages is a stile set by the end of the churchyard wall.

You now go uphill, half-right, towards the upper field corner; then the path leads on from the top stile, over grass, to reach the left side of the wood ahead. Keep to this pretty path with the wood now just on your right.

At a lane reached when the wood ends, go left past St Margaret's School for only 50 yards before turning in on the right at a marked path starting beside some cottages. The path soon breaks out into a fine grassy meadow and, following a left-hand hedge all the way, takes you downhill to reach a road at Nettleden, in half a mile.

Nettleden is one of Hertfordshire's smallest villages, on the edge of the Ashridge estate. St Lawrence's church, a nineteenth-century building, has an attractive approach with clipped yews. The tower is fifteenth-century.

Go past the church, but bear leftwards, just beyond, up a steep lane. This is a stiff climb, and the lane rises from below 400 feet (120 m) towards the ridge of 550 feet (170 m) in only a quarter of a mile. You will pass an iron gate on the right when you are almost at the top, and 80 yards beyond this, when you are virtually on level ground, take a path starting from a signposted stile on the right, set in the hedge. In the field beyond there are wonderful views again across the Gade valley. The path hugs the hedgeline (left) to a wood. Go straight ahead into the wood, by way of a stile, and swing leftwards under the canopy of the trees along the firm woodland way. (Many walkers say that this path is one of the finest in the county.)

It runs never far away from the wood's upper side, and after bending around a large hollow it continues until it starts to run downhill through the greenwood. You emerge from the wood to go even more steeply downhill until you reach a double stile, passed on your outward trip. Now cross and turn sharp left, following the path to the Cock and Bottle again.

5. Brookmans Park

Circular walk from Brookmans Park station by way of Abdale, North Mymms Park, Colney Heath Common, Ridge and Hawkshead Wood (South Mimms).

Start: Brookmans Park railway station.
Grid reference: TL 241040.
Distance: 9½ miles (15.3 km) or 7½ miles (12.1 km).
Ordnance Survey maps: 1:50,000 sheet 166; 1:25,000 sheet TL 20.

Normally spelt Mymms, in contrast to its neighbour South Mimms, North Mymms, in Hertfordshire, is set in amazingly rural country in the extreme south of the county. Here the scene is filled with the quiet of great woods — once part of the forest of Middlesex. The woods can make for muddy walking so do not tackle the walk in very damp conditions. You can get there and back by train (Eastern Region).

Leave Brookmans Park station, and turn in by the path that starts just beside the exit path at the bridge from the 'down' (away from London) side of the railway. You are soon in a field, with the station buildings just on your left.

When the path divides as the field widens, keep to the one skirting the right side. The hedgeside path leads to a corner at the far end, where it runs over a ditch to a clear path on the far side. Turn right to cross a stile at once and proceed with the wire fence on your right. At the end of the grassy field, turn right again at the corner over another stile. Now recross the ditch, and go leftwards on its far side by a broad track, known as Wise's Lane, which follows a tall wire fence (right) all the way to a lane at the Mimmshall Brook.

Cross the bridge into Watergate Road and, turning right, follow to a pedestrian bridge spanning the busy A1 main road. On its far side, work round the columns to the straight *dirt* track starting here, reached by a short path alongside the road fencing. After a full quarter of a mile, look out for a broad track meeting your way from the left: at this junction turn right along a sedate rural way that brings you up to an iron gate and stile. Cross and follow the path under the shade of occasional trees to another iron gate at the main drive through North Mymms Park. (You may shorten your walk at this point, as shown on the map, by turning left and picking up the directions at letter **A** below).

The main walk turns right; after 250 yards the drive is lined with a well kept holly hedge. When this ends, bear left (opposite a footpath to Water End) and proceed along the drive to North

Mymms church, which you will glimpse over the trees.

North Mymms Church (St Mary's) stands on the site of an earlier chapel. Visit it if you have time for there is a fine array of monuments including the altar tomb of Derbyshire alabaster in the window recess of the north aisle.

Leave the far side of the churchyard through the iron cage-wicket opposite the west door and strike *slightly* right to a gateside stile at the main drive to the house. Keeping your direction, cross to a sturdy plank bridge and so to stiles at a large rising meadow. Aim slightly right again, so that you 'clip' the projecting corner of the fencing on the right side of the field, and keep on over grassland so that you reach a stile in the perimeter fence of the park.

Now there is a less pleasant half-mile walk along the road to the left, uphill (although there are no footpaths, it is possible to gain the road higher up). You pass Tollgate Farm on your left, and after bearing left with the road reach the outskirts of Colney Heath. In another quarter of a mile there is a clear footpath (left) opposite Fellows Lane. This path runs beside the hedge over a field to cross a stream by a concrete bridge and on to a stile at a road.

Cross the road and go left to follow a border path along the road at the edge of Colney Heath Common. When it runs out to the road again at a bend, continue along the road to Coursers Farm on your left (the first driveway). Go along the drive, with the farm buildings on your left, and straight ahead by a concrete track through fields for over half a mile with the wooded ridges of North Mymms ahead. You will find the track turns at last and unpredictably expires at a concrete apron, with a choice of tracks. Take the left-hand one and follow it, at first with a ditch on its left. Later it goes right, then left, climbing up to finish at a field-gate by a large tree. Behind you are fine views across towards St Albans. Just before the gate, follow the hedgeline from this tree on your right along the top side of a field for 50 yards and, when the hedge swings away left, strike straight ahead over the rising ground (a line of stakes may be there to help you) to a stile in the upper field corner. The buildings of Radwell Wood Farm, marked by a large silo, can be glimpsed ahead.

Cross the stile and follow the hedge on your right up to the farm, then bear leftwards around the side of the field, bringing the buildings on your right, to the start of a clear wide (often muddy) track that leads away from the farm towards the woods. Follow it through gates and so over grass, parallel with a wood on the right of the field, and continue ahead to a gate near the far corner, in a line of hedgerow trees. Pass through, and

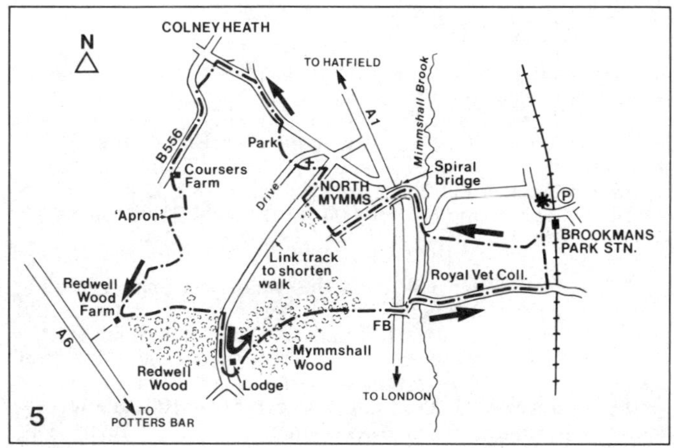

through the hedge gap a yard or so ahead, into a gently falling field with wide views over towards Brookmans Park. It is a very pretty rural prospect.

Go downhill now and, on striking the gravel drive at the bottom, bear right on it to pass a lonely cottage (**A**) and on through wonderful woods to the lodge at South Mimms (if you continue you will reach the village).

The walk, however, makes a sharp left turn to a bridleway (signed) which runs back into the woods and starts *immediately* beyond the lodge garden. This leads up through Mymmshall Wood and Hawkshead Wood and you simply follow the track all the way for three quarters of a mile and cross the A1 by a sweeping concrete footbridge.

Go left along the lane on the far side for 200 yards or so to the bridge at Hawkshead Lane (right). Cross the bridge and follow this lane, passing the Veterinary College, to a metalled path on the left before a bridge. This runs beside the railway line and leads back in half a mile to Brookmans Park station.

6. Watton-at-Stone

Circular walk from Watton-at-Stone (or Bull's Green) by way of Queen Hoo and Bramfield.

Start: Watton-at-Stone railway station (or Bull's Green).
Grid reference: TL 298192 (station) or TL 272172 (Bull's Green).
Distance: 7 miles (11.3 km) or 5¼ miles (8.5 km).
Ordnance Survey maps: 1:50,000 sheet 166; 1:25,000 sheet TL 21.

Queen Hoo Hall, passed on this walk, was once a hunting lodge of Queen Elizabeth I, and it lies in rolling and beautiful country that is quite close to London. The starting point for the full walk is Watton-at-Stone station, reopened in the 1980s after closure in 1939. The station is at the village. For those who prefer a shorter walk, the route has been designed to allow for a start to be made at the tiny hamlet of Bull's Green, near Datchworth.

From Watton-at-Stone station, on the Datchworth Road, cross the road to a lane opposite the station entrance and, after following it for 200 yards, go right by a track leading to Watkins Hall, the farmhouse clearly visible ahead.

Pass the farm and cross the gate 150 yards ahead, where tracks lead left and forward. Select the forward track, which runs gently uphill over fine open country, following a hedge (right) for some way. After a twist, the track reaches the top of the long rise at a hedge. Here go right with the main path, and then, after about 50 yards, you will find that the path runs across the field in your original direction, roughly towards a concrete water tower. On reaching a wide rough track, go right along it for some yards in the direction of the tower, then go left along a pleasant track when you reach the boundary fencing, to keep the fenced area on your right hand. Soon you will break out into a road, where you should go right until it reaches Bull's Green crossroads, just ahead.

Bull's Green consists of little more than the green itself, with a few houses and the Horns inn, set in very rural country. It is set in the large forested area known as Bramfield Forest. The Horns, a pretty little inn with a well earned reputation for food, staged the final act in a drama of the eighteenth century. There was wild rejoicing here when a local farmer reported the death of the footpad Clibborn in 1782. Clibborn was a pie-man (like Simple Simon), who frequented Hertford market and afterwards, in the depths of Bramfield Forest,

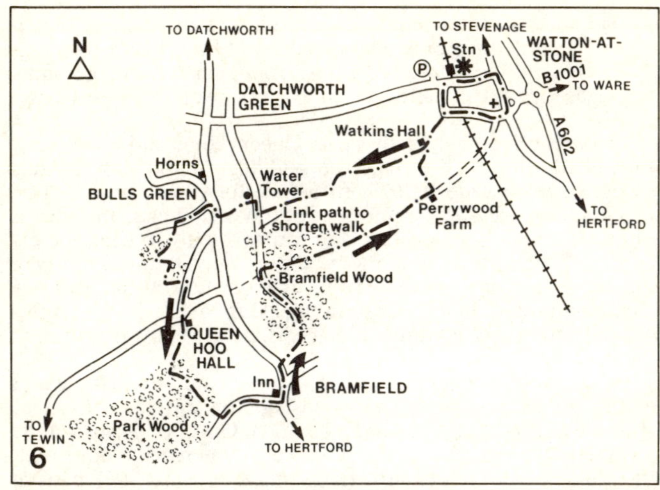

waylaid farmers who had successfully sold their produce. Clibborn's Post, on the roadside near Queen Hoo, is periodically replaced; it marks the spot where the footpad's body was riven by a stake, in the barbarous fashion of the times.

From Bull's Green (the starting point for walkers who prefer the shorter distance), take the road signposted to Burnham Green (*not* the road beside the petrol station). After 250 yards, look for the long drive to number 27, just beyond a house called Trevence; a few yards beyond this point on your left side there is a signposted stile that marks the start of a path running along the boundary fencing of this property. Follow the path by the fencing until it wanders out through a belt of woodland.

It runs clearly on, just inside the edge of the wood, with the fields on your left. Later, the path winds leftwards and uphill before swinging round to the right again with woods on your left. At the end of the wood line, the fieldpath strikes a line of heavy fencing; go left here to keep the woods on your left, until you run out in 250 yards at a lonely lane, near a house on your left. Turn right along the lane, passing another lane that reaches you from the left, and continue for a short way to a point just ahead where the lane turns sharp right at the driveway to Queen Hoo Hall.

Queen Hoo Hall is said to be a hunting lodge that dates back to early Elizabethan times; its unusual design suggests that it was intended for only occasional use. Mural figure paintings of that period adorn an upper room, and from the small terraced garden there are fine views over the Lea valley.

Leave the lane at the drive to Queen Hoo, and go directly forward by the track to pass the building on your left. It runs straight over a wide field, with wonderful views ahead. Upon reaching the edge of Bramfield Park Wood ahead, the way is often cut up by horses; however, you have only to continue for another 200 yards or so along it before you will discover a gate on the left, with a stile (there is also a notice by the Forestry Commission prohibiting horse riding along the track). Cross this gateside stile, and continue along this clear wide track through the wood.

At the far end, where you reach another gate, turn left beyond it and go along a lane that leads up towards the village of Bramfield, on the rise ahead of you. The Granison Arms will be passed on the left, and shortly afterwards you reach Main Road, the village street. Here turn left along the road. After passing the lane to Stapleford on your right, keep along the road for another 200 yards and look for a broad grassy track also on your right hand, marked with a path sign. It runs gently up towards the distant trees. Go along it towards the wood, soon with trees on either side. This is Bramfield Wood, much reduced in size from Clibborn's day, but still impressive. As you keep along this wide trackway into the woods you may note a pathway coming in from the right; this has come from the Stapleford Road.

The track, as it explores the wood, runs always ahead, after some way gently curving towards the left. Ignore any tiny paths on the right of your wide grassy way and, after almost half a mile from the point where you first entered the woodlands, look out for a wide crossing track. Still carry on over this track, and in another 500 yards you will reach another wide cross track; here a tree has been arranged across the way to act as a jump for horses. Continue ahead, still, for 150 yards to a third crossing track in these popular woods; you should find a wooden footway sign bearing numbers nearby, a product of the county council's efforts to encourage the public to use country paths. *At this point walkers who wish to end their day at Bull's Green on the short route should continue along Back Lane, as this wide track we have followed is known, until the water tower is reached in another 600 yards, before turning left along the boundary fencing to reach the road, then turning right along it (signed towards Datchworth) to Bull's Green crossroads again.*

The main walk returns to Watton-at-Stone from the crossing track by a right turn along the smaller track. (In winter you will be able to spot a small pond on the left almost at once, but in summertime this little clue is well shielded by the greenery.) After only 150 yards along this new track you will emerge at a track junction, with a good track on the left, whilst just ahead are open fields. (If you walk the few yards to the open, you will discover some open views over the wide, shallow valley towards the Woodhall Park.)

Take this track on your left hand — it has a Forestry Commission board (dogs on lead) at its head. This path runs through the wooded area, making its way gradually downhill, and soon the wide open farmland parallel to the path disappears from sight behind the trees. The gently falling path finally breaks out, in some 400 yards, to the field track on the right which has been also running downhill on the far side of the wood.

Continue now along the field track downhill all the way to Perrywood Farm, and after passing the black wooden barns go sharply left, after a further 80 yards, along a signposted bridleway running through trees. On reaching a field, keep ahead to the farm gate at Watkins Hall, and pass through it and on beyond the farm to reach the railway again.

You can visit Watton's fine old church and see the village by continuing ahead over the railway bridge opposite the farm track. To reach the station you go left, along your outward route, at the end of the Watkins Hall track.

Watton-on-Stone is said to have got its name from a milestone that once may have stood beside the Waggon and Horses, at the north end of the village. The mill on the river Beane was mentioned in Domesday. The church (St Andrew and St Mary) is prettily surrounded by trees; some fine memorials to the Boteler family may be seen inside.

7. Offley

Circular walk from Offley by way of Offleydown, Charlton and Offley Bottom (with alternative start and finish at Hitchin).

Start: Offley, Green Man public house (or Hitchin, St Mary's Square).
Grid reference: TL 143271 (Offley) or TL 187291 (Hitchin).
Distance: 6 miles (9.7 km).
Ordnance Survey maps: 1:50,000 sheet 166; 1:25,000 sheet TL 12.

The Salusbury family lived, during the eighteenth century, at Offley Place, a fine mansion in Offley village, between Hitchin and Luton. The house, a few miles inside Hertfordshire, still stares eastwards over a gentle wide vale, watered by tiny springs that lie enclosed by the eastern folds of the Chilterns. This undemanding walk is over rich farmland, which is still, apart from the elms and the hedgerow losses, much as it must have looked two centuries ago when Sir Thomas Salusbury and his spirited young niece (Dr Johnson's Mrs Thrale) lived here.

The walk starts from the village centre, at the top of Offley Hill, at the Green Man public house.

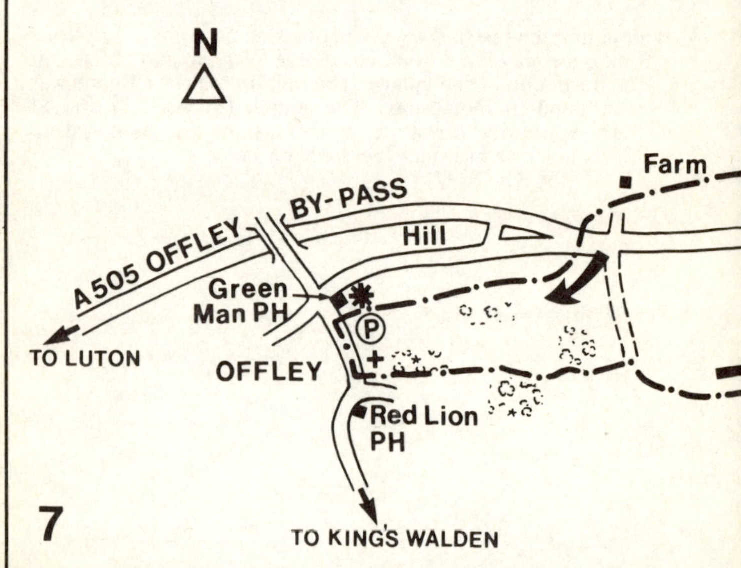

Walk along the lane towards Offley church, noting Offley Place on your left. Turn left on the footpath starting from a stile at the churchyard's far boundary.

The footpath soon breaks into a field ahead. The way is forward (but you will find it sensible to move a few yards leftwards into the belt of trees and follow a wandering path under their shade as they line the side of the field, until it turns into the field again). Still keep ahead by a track as the ground falls between a screen of trees. In the lower field, the path still hugs the treeline along the right side. At the lower part, as the treeline breaks, strike across the width of the field, and on by a path that now has trees on its left, running up to a corner stile. Cross and, with the hedge on your right, keep on the path as it twists down to a rutty track that runs left to a broad crossing track at the bottom of the hills. (Away to your left you will hear the traffic roar on the A505.)

Turn squarely right, keeping along this pleasant rural way through fields (here and there it has been enclosed by wire to restrict horse riders). In half a mile or so it crosses another bold track. Continue straight ahead over a field to pick up the hedgeline in the distance, and, keeping this on your left hand, carry on. The ground, as the path matures into a wide enclosed track, is now elevated, affording some splendid pastoral views to

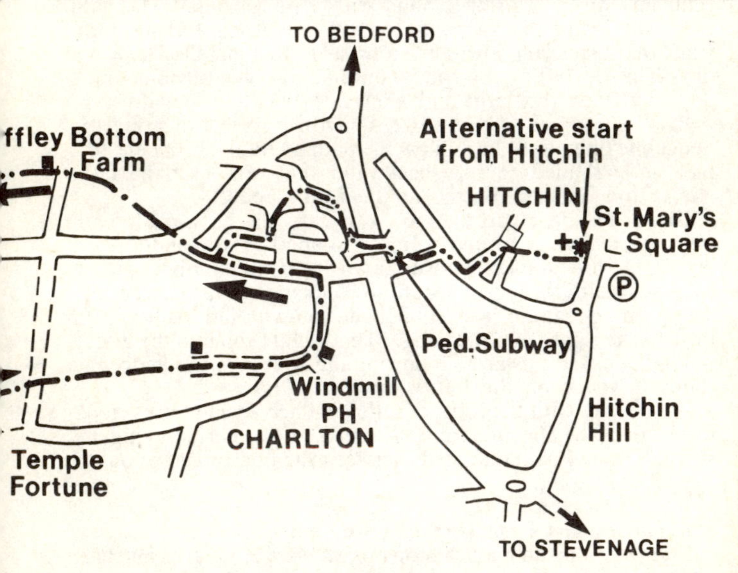

the south. The gentle valley on the right was the proposed route of the Hitchin West Railway in 1889, a light railway intended to link Hitchin and Luton, via Offley Hill. It would have necessitated a tunnel of 1127 feet (344 m) through Offley Hill (which you will see later), a fact that must have forced the abandonment of the project. When the track ends at a cottage, go downhill by a metalled lane and turn left at whitewashed cottages to Charlton village. (As you go downhill from the upper cottage, you may see, left, at the end of the garden a small brick ruin; this was the base of old Charlton windmill.)

Keep along the lane to a junction in half a mile (Willow Lane). (Here, on the outskirts of Hitchin, you may break your walk to reach the town by turning right, passing under the bypass by the subway to the town centre.)

The main walk continues by a left turn at Willow Lane for half a mile to the Luton Road. (The lane, though wooded, is narrow and twisty so care is needed: a good idea is to walk up the first road on the right (Hawthorn Close), turn left and walk along an estate road, rejoining Willow Lane by taking the next turn left.) At the Luton Road (A505) **(X)** cross to a signposted footpath starting from the field-gate opposite. It follows the remains of a hedgeline (left) that has been mangled by excessive pruning by farm machinery. At the end, go through a gap a yard or so to the right and on over rising ground with a hedge (left). The path then runs, with the hedgeline on your right, to a vague farm track that takes you down, in a few yards, to a metalled lane in a dip. This is Offley Bottom; continue by the obvious track opposite, past the farm and alongside the field ahead.

In a quarter of a mile move a yard or so left to bring the hedgeline on your right. Follow the path on until it broadens to a pleasantly shaded country backwater that runs past the farm ahead and on to a V stile at the Luton road.

Cross this dual carriageway with care to the asphalt path opposite that runs around cottages to another stile and a road. Now go to a field-gate opposite, a few yards to the right, and on by a clear path through a beautiful woodland glade to a clearing. The path appears to lead uphill, but you will find a stile just a little to the right, near the hedge. This admits you into the grassy field ahead. Go upwards, following the course of the hedgeline (later a wood) on the left.

At the top, with the roofs of Offley village again in view, look for a stile some 50 yards from the field's left corner, marking the start of a small path that leads between the houses and so out to the village street.

Alternative start from Hitchin town centre

From the bus and coach stops in St Mary's Square, Hitchin,

walk towards the market and, with the church on your right, continue to Market Place. Cross to Bucklersbury, a small street leading off the square, by the Freeman Hardy and Willis shoe shop. At the end of Bucklersbury, go right up Tilehouse Street, first left along Old Charlton Lane and straight ahead to go under the bypass by a subway. Continue ahead past flats and pedestrian guard rails at the start of a side road (garages). Go along the road towards the large block of flats ahead, pass it on your right, but keep *forward* to a white cottage at Russell's Slip (pedestrian passage). Go left to a green and road (Cranbourne Avenue). Turn right now for a quarter mile to a downhill turn on the left leading out to Willow Lane, and turn right to Luton Road. Now follow the walk from point **(X)** in the main walk.

8. Wheathampstead

Circular walk from Wheathampstead by way of Lamer Park, Ayot St Lawrence and Water End.

Start: Wheathampstead, main street.
Grid reference: TL 178140.
Distance: 8 miles (12.9 km).
Ordnance Survey maps: 1:50,000 sheet 166; 1:25,000 sheet TL 17.

By the upper waters of the river Lea cattle browse in the lush meadows that provide the setting for the last stages of this walk. Earlier, we explore the fields around the secluded village of Ayot St Lawrence, which the playwright George Bernard Shaw made his home.

From the main street of Wheathampstead, walk downhill past the Bull (on your right) and up to the roundabout. (You will see here a stone on the right recording that this was the site of the old railway station on the Hatfield, Luton and Dunstable railway from 1860 until 1965. You will pass under its course later.)

Go along the road directly opposite (Lamer Lane) and follow it gently uphill, past some farm buildings. After 500 yards you reach a drive on your right marking the lodge gates of Lamer Park; turn right along it, past the lodge, and go along this fine drive through some beautiful parkland, with a strong stand of firs on your right. On higher ground continue past a cottage (left) and on by the drive (which has now lost its surface) to pass Lamer House, on the left.

Lamer Park was the home of Aspley Cherry-Garrard, Antarctic explorer with Scott. He went on a midwinter journey with Dr

Wilson, who perished with Scott, in search of Emperor penguins. He told the story of the expedition in *The Worst Journey in the World.*

Just beyond the house, bear right at a track fork (but observe the pretty stable block on the left) and on by a fine avenue of limes. There are some very fine ancient trees in this part of the park: an example is the old sweet chestnut tree standing alone in the field on the right. When the drive reaches the end of the second field, leave it for the left-hand hedge-lined footway that you will find starting at a stile and five-bar gate just to your left, near the field corner. Soon you emerge in a remote little lane, which you should follow to the right, towards the village of Ayot St Lawrence.

In 200 yards, look for an iron swing-gate on your left, at the drive to the 'new' Ayot St Lawrence church. Here, it is worth a short diversion along the drive to the church.

From the iron swing-gate at the lane, go into the field and then slightly right over grass, aiming for the white cottage on the far side. The path will lead through sturdy timber gates and between wire fencing to reach it. You will arrive at another gate beside the cottage. Here, at the lane, you will see the village centre, with its ruined church and the pub called the Brocket Arms on your left. The course of the walk, however, is now to the right along the lane; at a road fork at the first bend keep forward (i.e. left) with Shaw's House, owned by the National Trust, on your right.

This lane soon swings round a bend to the left; leave it when it swings right in a few more yards, and follow a track starting ahead of you, on the left side of the road. This track runs at first between hedges (which can make for muddy walking during wet weather) up to higher ground. It is a bridleway and gets cut up by horses, so that you may find you can follow its course over the fields by using footpaths to its left (i.e. on the far side of the hedge). Follow its direction through a small wood and later, when the track starts to run downhill, you can cross to the left side and wander through a long narrow copse (known as Stocking Spring) which lines the left side of the track. Soon you reach a gate and a small lane at a bend.

Continue up the track opposite. With a wood for a long time on the left, the track (with fine views away to the right) eventually curves leftwards to run through a section of the wood and along the left-hand side of one field and the right-hand side of a second to pass under the brick arch of the old railway mentioned earlier.

The Ayot Greenway. The track bed of the disused Luton,

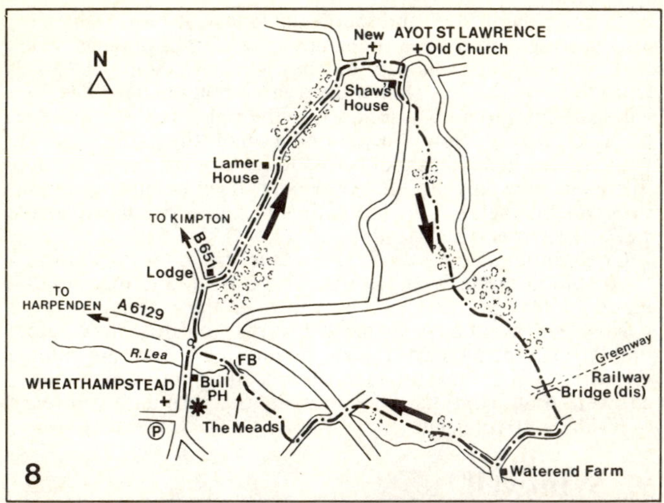

Dunstable and Welwyn Junction Railway is now open to the public as the Ayot Greenway. There is a walking and riding route along the section cleared for use, and the county authorities hope to develop the wildlife habitats found along its length.

The way continues under the bridge and along the track running beside the right side of a field to reach a lane at a bend, where you go right. Follow the lane as it winds to drop at last downhill to the ford at Water End.

Water End Farm (left, just before the river), is a red-brick Jacobean manor house with fine decorated chimneys. It is generally considered that Sarah Jennings (1660-1744), the formidable Duchess of Marlborough and friend of Queen Anne, was born here. The house was built for her father, John.

Turn right, opposite the house, and go along the wide track now designated as the River Lea Walk (with the swan emblem). Keep straight ahead when the track turns right, and go on beside the wide river, with the sparkling water to your left. Keep on, over a stile, and later follow a line of electricity poles through a perfect water meadow; when the hedge on the left drops away, keep ahead to strike a tiny lane, with a bypass road and bridge just to your left. Here the original path has been diverted, so go left, under the bridge, and follow the lane as it turns right, then left, passing a handful of bungalows and farm buildings. Look for a narrow but clear path on the right here, some 200 yards from the bridge. This is lined by a large holly hedge. The path will lead out into a field; follow it to the right, skirting the edge, to the far corner. Now you will find a small stile in the hedge on your right, which you should cross to go forward again, keeping the hedge now on your left. Away over the grass on your right is the river Lea again. This footpath is part of a popular riverside walk known as The Meads.

Cross another stile ahead into another field. Go forward to a third stile in the left-hand corner of the field, and then on to a metal footbridge, which takes you over the water.

Now go by the path half-leftwards towards the factory buildings on the outskirts of Wheathampstead. The path you are following will join a broader track leading leftwards along a concrete road; continue forward along the path until you reach the village street again.

9. Whitwell

Circular walk from Whitwell by way of Stagenhoe Park, Preston End, Chapelfoot, Minsden Chapel and St Paul's Walden.

Start: Whitwell High Street.
Grid reference: TL 183211.
Distance: 7½ miles (12.1 km).
Ordnance Survey maps: 1:50,000 sheet 166; 1:25,000 sheet TL 12.

This is royal country, in every sense. The views are on a grand scale on this mid Hertfordshire walk, and you will pass through St Paul's Walden Park, the estate where the Queen Mother was born in August 1900. You will also visit the romantic ruins of Minsden Chapel, perched on a lonely hillside.

From Whitwell High Street walk west to pass the Bull and the Maiden's Head (on your left) and continue past road junctions on the left and some pleasant watercress beds on the right (the plant grows well here in the constantly moving waters of the Minram). As the lane turns just beyond the watercress, turn right along the field track signposted to Preston. It runs uphill, framed with occasional hedgerow trees. Follow the drive through a second field, with a wood on your left and, away to your right, a surprise view of the stuccoed and pedimented Stagenhoe Park mansion.

Stagenhoe was rebuilt after a fire in the early nineteenth century

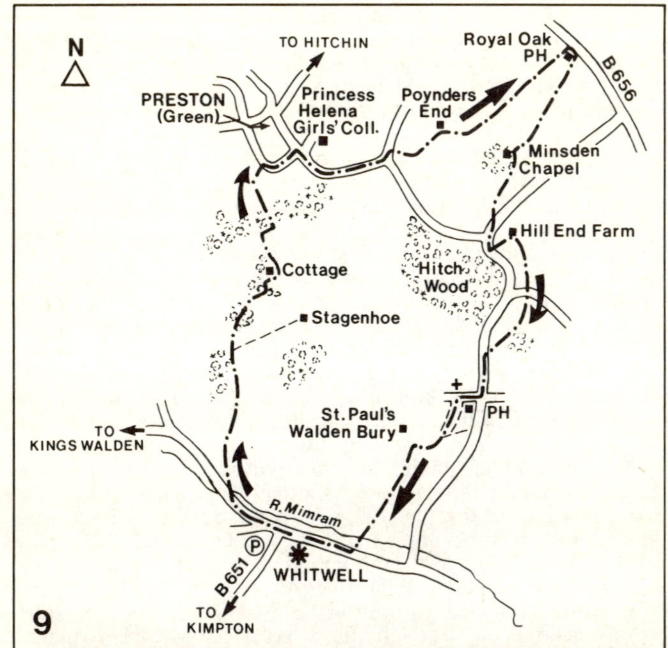

(this was a common happening in the age of candlelight). The earlier house was said to have been linked to nearby Temple Disney by a secret underground passage. The house's finest days were when the Caithness family lived there. The Earl of Caithness was delightfully eccentric: he rode (with difficulty) around the nearby rutted lanes in a one-wheeled conveyance of his own invention. Stagenhoe is now a Sue Ryder home.

On reaching a cross drive, keep forward by a path whose course is marked by hedgerow trees. You will be led towards a wood, and the way is through the outer edge of the wood to reach a stile at a field. Continue now besides a right-hand hedge, and through another small wood to emerge in quiet pasture, with the footpath curving away leftwards to follow the line of the wood towards a pretty red-tiled cottage at a track. Turn left, to pass the cottage front, and go downhill towards the small clump of trees in the centre of fields. Turn at the tree clump and, keeping it on your right, go right, uphill, following the hedgeline to a large wood, but do not venture into it. Instead, turn right again, following the path skirting the wood, now on your left.

200 yards or so from the turn, there is an iron cage-wicket set back in the hedge on the left to allow you to enter the wood. (This gate is some 50 yards beyond the prominent tree that juts a little way out into the field.) Although it was clearly marked with a board when surveyed, the growth of high summer is such that care is needed here.

Passing through the cage-wicket, continue by the clear path through the wood, with a dark stand of firs to your left and oaks to the right. The clear path later runs beside a hedge, with fields on your right, passes another little gate and reaches a wider, overgrown fieldway, where the footpath swings clearly right for another 150 yards to reach a metalled driveway at a bend. Here keep straight forward, down and up a small dip to another small lane intersection, where you bear right; this leads quickly to a T junction at the gates of the Princess Helena College (a private girls' school). Turn right yet again along the road. The college buildings were once known as Temple Disney and were the home of the McMillian family. The house had connections with a religious order, and many legends are woven around it.

Keep on for a long half mile to a T junction. Here turn left for 20 yards and take the signposted footpath on the right side of the road. For a short distance the path, which runs beside the wire fencing of a water pumping station, can be narrow and tricky with summer overgrowth, but you are soon out in a wide field, which you skirt along its right edge. As the path turns beyond the field corner, it changes to run with the hedge on your left side, soon reaching, on your left, the wonderful old timber-framed farmhouse of Poynders End, which looks across the long valley. The way continues down, with the Minsden ruins away to your right, all the way to the main Welwyn road near the Royal Oak (just to your right) at Chapelfoot.

On the far side of the inn, a signposted bridleway starting from the car park will take you uphill again, beside hedges all the way, to the triangular skeleton of the Minsden chapel, which is framed against the sky.

Minsden was once a chapel of ease for Hitchin, and the ruins provide the last resting place for the historian Reginald Hine, whose tomb slab may be seen in the chapel. The last wedding at the chapel (popular because of its romantic setting) was performed in 1738, when some masonry fell down, narrowly missing the happy couple.

Leave the chapel on your right, and follow the track beside the trees down to the Whitwell road. Continue to the right for a few dozen yards and look for a bridleway, which you will find on the left at the corner. Turn left up it to Hillend Farm, turning right off this farm road once you have passed the main buildings. (Do *not* bear left with the road beyond it.) Go straight ahead at this point by a small track leading to the field above the farm. Beyond a metal gate the track continues, with the hedge right, along uphill pasture, then swings right on reaching the far field corner to reveal a painted swing-gate. After this, the path wobbles left and right enclosed by hedges until you reach a tiny lane.

Keep your direction straight across the lane and cross via a wooden rail on the far side into a large field. From here the way runs directly across to pass just right of the wood ahead (ignore the large woodland away on the right). During most of the year you should find no problem crossing this field; in high summer, if the crops are grown tall, you may prefer to skirt around via the fencing on the left. If you keep a straight course over the field you can cross a stile at the wooded area (here just on your left), or if you skirt around you will pass the side of the wood before reaching this stile. Continue from the stile in the same straight direction to reach woods at the top of a hill (you will hear the sound of traffic climbing the hill on your right). Go through the small band of trees to reach the road, where you turn left along it from the brow of the hill.

Almost at once you pass the lodge gates of Stagenhoe Park. The road goes downhill to the crossroads and the Strathmore Arms (on your right). Turn right up the tiny lane beside the pub to the church, then swing leftwards downhill by the track directly opposite. You will pass a Victorian Gothick cottage on the left, almost at the start of a metalled drive.

The drive takes you uphill to the right, before it widens to turn towards the red-brick mansion of St Paul's Walden Bury, where the Queen Mother was born on 4th August 1900.

As the drive turns, look for an iron cage-wicket on the left; go through it into parkland. Now go downhill all the way following the line of ancient trees, and on, through another iron gate, to reach the river Mimram, which is crossed at this point by a misshapen concrete bridge.

Just ahead is a stile which brings you out into the village street of Whitwell again.

10. Hitchin

Circular walk from Hitchin by way of Austage End and King's Walden.
Start: Hitchin, St Mary's Square.
Grid reference: TL 187291.
Distance: 11 miles (17.8 km).
Ordnance Survey maps: 1:50,000 sheet 166; 1:25,000 sheet TL 12.

This is a very pleasant day's walk amid the Chiltern folds of north Hertfordshire. The country is beautiful in all seasons and, although so near Luton, there is a tumble of hills and dales, with very little road walking.

Hitchin, still a market town, retains its medieval plan. The town market is held on Tuesdays and Saturdays on land at the side of St Mary's Square. Note the Biggin Almshouses, a timber-framed building, as you walk along Queen Street. Henry VIII had a narrow escape when in Hitchin, fleeing in his night clothes from a fire at the Angel Inn (now demolished) in Sun Street, St Mary's church is one of the finest in the county. St Mary's Square was fashioned from an early slum clearance scheme of the 1920s, one of the most advanced town planning projects of its day.

From the bus terminus at St Mary's Square, with the telephone exchange on the far side of the road, turn right to pass the Bricklayers' Arms and continue along Queen Street, bearing up Hitchin Hill at the Lister House Hotel. Near the top of the rise, after walking along the *right*-hand side of the road, bear right with a blind lane and continue over the concrete pedestrian bridge crossing the bypass (Priory Way). After crossing, take the swing-gate on the right at once, and go along the footpath that skirts the boundary of the road at first, then turns leftwards to run across Priory Park. The broad path dips, then rises; it is worth a glance behind you to see Hitchin Priory.

Hitchin Priory is now owned by an insurance group, after some years as a county council property. The last private owners, the Delmé-Radcliffe family, left in 1963. The house was founded on the site of an old Carmelite priory, which dated from 1317. The front which you see is the south front, erected in 1771 in the style of Robert Adam. Adam had drawn up plans for a new mansion a short distance away, but they proved to be too expensive to realise.

Look for a side path on the right at the top of the field rise and take it to reach a stile overlooking the village of Charlton. (Do not worry if you miss it: simply continue to a lane then turn

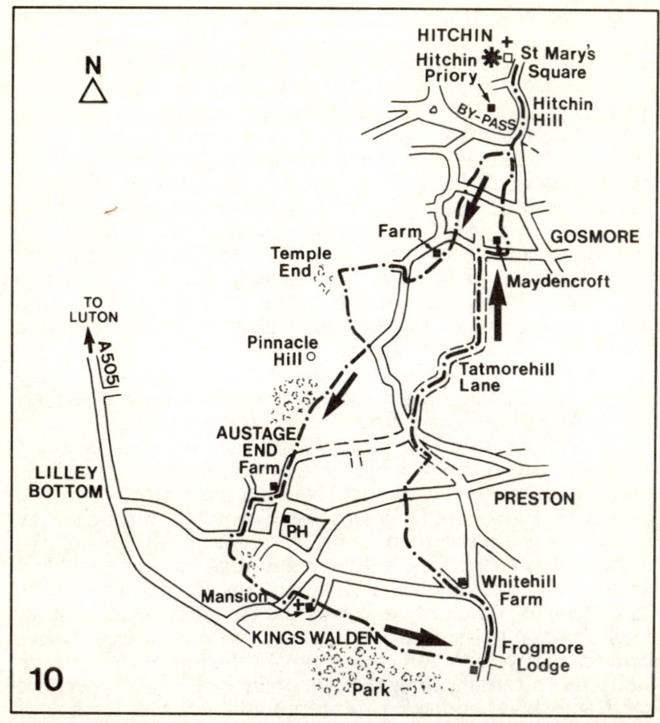

downhill to Charlton.) The path runs, enclosed, down to a lane, with a large white thatched cottage ahead (and the main village away to the right). Continue over the lane with the cottage on your left and, when the lane turns right at a farm, keep forward to a field-gate and stile ahead. (On your right is old Charlton watermill, shielded by the fence.) Go ahead over grass along the lower part of two fields to reach a white cottage at a sharp bend; cross into the field corner directly ahead, and keep the hedge near your right hand to pass above a farm (right) and on, in line with slight undulations that are all that remains of a fine hedgerow, until a lane is reached in half a mile. Now go downhill to the right for 30 yards, then left along a 'no through road'. Beyond some straggling settlements the lane loses its surface and reaches the edge of a wood at Temple End.

Turn sharply left at the trees, bringing them on your right as you follow an attractive path, here and there enclosed with hedges, which rises gently to break out into open land at last on either side. Persevere as the path turns into a cart track and runs up to a sharp road bend, with cottages ahead.

Avoiding the road, make a right turn over a gate and walk uphill beside the left side of a field; away to the right is the high ground known as Pinnacle Hill with a ring of trees. The iron fencing leads to a gate and a small path through a wood. On the far side the path continues up the valley, at first with an iron fence on your left, then a few bushes, so that you reach a corner gate. Now the path rises more steeply between trees and continues, enclosed by wire, along the left side of a wood and over a crossing track. The clear path ahead follows the side of a field for 50 yards, bears slightly left and broadens into a rutted track running on to a hedge gap ahead. Go through the gap and keep beside a hedge to emerge at cottages at a remote country spot known as Austage End.

Now walk forward along the lane to reach the main lane at a crossing near a farm. Turn right at this crossroads. On reaching a T junction turn left to walk south before turning right at a second T junction. Now look for a signposted footpath starting on the opposite side of the road, some 15 yards or so beyond the junction. It starts from a field gap and runs beside a left-hand hedge, giving fine views over Lilley Bottom. Bear leftwards with the hedgeline and carry on to pass the tall storage barn ahead. After another 100 yards, upon reaching a band of trees, leave the track that you are now on and follow the line of the trees on your right by turning along the side of the field. Again there are wonderful views, and again you turn to the left with the line of the wood in 100 yards. As the path turns, King's Walden church can be seen ahead. Continue by the hedgeside path to reach the road at a gate near the church.

King's Walden is little more than a huddle of cottages serving the estate house of The Bury. The church is attractively perched on high ground. The land was owned by the king at the time of Domesday, but its later owners, the Hale family, continued here from Elizabethan times until the twentieth century. In 1890 the old manor house was taken down. The present house, seen soon, dates from 1955. St Mary's church has a vestry built in 1680, as a burial place for the Hales. Richard Pike and William Upward were two King's Walden men who fought at Agincourt.

Move several yards up the road to the left, to a signposted stile on the right, cross and strike forward over grass, setting a course roughly parallel to the boundary hedging of the cottage on the right. As you go, you will soon have a fine view of the manor on your right. A straight line will bring you to an elderly iron cage-wicket at a fine approach avenue to the house. Cross directly to the stile remains opposite, and follow the line of fencing on your left for almost a mile over some very fine grassland dotted with great oaks, which are beyond their prime. This is a grand walk and will lead you out, along a drive, at the far lodge gates at Frogmore Bottom.

Turn left up the hill to pass a side road on the right about 200 yards after reaching the top. Pass Whitehill Farm immediately, and at once take the 'no through road' on the right, by the side of the farm. This leads past a cottage or two of enviable quaintness before the track reaches a small wood and dies away into a staggered series of ruts leading to the field beyond. Here you will find the bridleway swings sharp right, plunging downhill through bushes running along the side of the field. At the bottom of the valley you emerge into the open, and then the clear path leads upward to a lane, which you cross directly, proceeding now along a level gravel track that runs ahead as far as you can see with a hedge on the left. At the end of the first field keep forward for another 250 yards to strike a wide broad green lane, known as Dead Woman's Lane, which comes in from your right. This green lane will lead you, by turning left along it, out to a road beside a cottage.

Now cross the road obliquely to the wide track ahead. This is another Hertfordshire green lane. It is called Tatmorehill Lane and will take you on for over half a mile, with an occasional small twist, until it turns to run downhill with increasing steepness, emerging into the open and giving you fine views towards Hitchin.

After another half mile the way runs out into a lane near the top of a hill. Turn right now, passing Maydencroft Farm, the grand old half-timbered mansion on your left, built in an L shape and now restored.

A short distance beyond, start looking for a signposted stile on the left side of the lane. Cross and follow the side of a field that skirts the boundary of the property. After passing forward through a small copse the path bends slightly left over grass to a stile by an oak, and then carries on, enclosed by wire around a field, to reach a stile at a lane. Cross over to an enclosed path to an estate road, go slightly left over the green to another enclosed path running between the houses opposite and, upon reaching Priory Park at a stile, let the path take you half-right towards the chestnuts on the right. Avoid the lodge exit and bear left under the trees all the way until you reach the pedestrian footbridge over the Hitchin bypass, here rejoining your outward route.

11. Ashwell

Circular walk from Ashwell by way of Hinxworth House, Hinxworth and Ashwell End.

Start: Ashwell church.
Grid reference: TL 267398.
Distance: 7½ miles (12.1 km)
Ordnance Survey maps: 1:50,000 sheet 153; 1:25,000 sheet TL 23.

On this walk we are in different countryside that hardly seems to represent Hertfordshire; near the Cambridgeshire border the skies are broad and wide, the fields reach upwards and there are few trees. Beloved of artists, this expansive country calls for a love of breezes and open air, for there is little shelter.

Ashwell. Few Hertfordshire villages have such charm. Cottages and pubs grouped around the church, with its lofty spire that will provide you with guidance throughout the walk, combine to make this prosperous place a haven for photographers and artists. St Mary's church is famous for the medieval graffiti, some mentioning the Black Death, on the west wall of the tower and on some of the nave columns.

There is plenty of parking space around the church; from here set out along Swan Street to gain the High Street (note the timber-framed Museum House on the way). Walk along the High Street towards the right; this will lead you to the west end of the village (it is also called that on a street name). Just beyond the main houses the road divides, with a road continuing ahead towards Newnham, and a right fork known as Hinxworth Road. Take the Hinxworth Road to pass West Point (a house), and keep straight ahead as the lane curves, to go gently uphill by a broad field track that follows a hedge on its left. In a mile, as the track descends, you will see a crossing hedgeline (hedges are very rare in this countryside). The track bears right at this point, keeping the hedge on your left. Ahead you will spot an ancient house: this is Hinxworth Place, your next objective. When the track sweeps away right, keep on beside the hedge towards the house. Just before the path reaches it, however, you walk beside a deep ditch flanking the property — once a defensive moat. You may also see sculptures in the garden (it is the home of an artist) before the very interesting east front of the Place comes into view.

Hinxworth Place is reputed to be haunted. A monk is said to

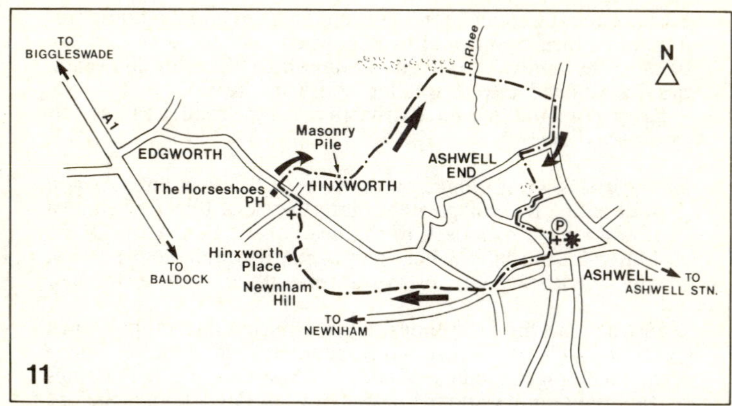

have been buried alive in the interior walls of this house, which was built about 1420 and may have been used as a retreat by monks from Nottinghamshire. Its interior is now partitioned into two separate units but the monk's ghost passes through the panelling and continues to walk along its original passages. Ghostly cries have also been heard, thought to be those of a baby who was the victim of a childish prank when its parents were worshipping at Hinxworth church across the fields. You may be able to glimpse the strong central door with its surrounding stone panels of great age.

Immediately behind the main building, leave the track and go through an iron gateway into the field on the right, and follow the line of a small straggle of trees and bushes into the field. When it ends in 50 yards or so, pause to look for the tower of Hinxworth church, half-left across the fields near the tops of some white farm buildings. The church provides the next objective in this walk; the old 'churchway' goes almost directly to it (in summer it may be easier to skirt around the field to the left). On arriving at a point where the hedge ends, move a little to the right to follow the line of a drainage dyke whilst still roughly heading towards the church, so that you pass the white farm buildings just to your left. On reaching the far side of the field, follow the hedge for a short distance to reach a wooden swing-gate leading into the churchyard itself. St Nicholas's church is usually kept locked, but note, as you wander around to the left of the church, the raised tomb slabs at the corner of the building marking the graves of the Sale family of Hinxworth

Place. The long connection between the Sales and the house was noted in a local newspaper in 1939 when 'the last representative of the Sale family, who lived in Hinxworth Place for 250 years, has just moved into a smaller house in the village'.

Keep along the tree-lined drive to reach the road, and turn left into the village.

Hinxworth is a tiny village on the edge of Bedfordshire. As you walk along the village steet, note the clock tower given as a useful village memorial to the dead of the First World War. Major Clutterbuck, whose name appears on the tower, was a member of the old Hertfordshire family of local historians.

Just beyond the Horsehoes, a pretty little thatched pub, turn right along Chapel Lane, to see some attractive houses and a farm, including the village pond. At the far end, the track swings to the right and wanders past a few isolated houses before dropping in a straight line over the fields. On reaching a broad cross track, (presently marked with a large pile of masonry), go leftwards along it as it crosses the open landscape. Away to the right you will glimpse the spire of Ashwell church. The track keeps straight (ignore a turning off towards a barn) for almost a mile until it reaches a band of trees, where it turns at last under their shade to the right. The trees sheltering the track here may make ground conditions a little muddy in wet weather, but you will soon cross a stream (the Rhee, one of the sources of the river Cam) and find that the way becomes a broad and open trackway that follows a line of strong fieldside trees to reach a lane, where you turn right. Turn right again at the first side road, and walk on for about a quarter of a mile to pass a house (left). At the far end of the property, you will find a stile on the left, marked with a footpath sign. Cross the stile and keep forward; when the fencing ends, continue across the grass on a straight course (ignoring the tracking made by horses). You aim for the small wood in the distance. Cross a stile in wire before you reach the wood, which you pass on your right, to reach a bar stile at a lane near Ashwell. Now go right, then left at a junction, and continue to head towards Ashwell church, until you reach the village again. A left fork at the village leads directly to the church.

12. Little Hadham

Circular walk from Little Hadham by way of Hadham Ford, Much Hadham, Bury Green and Church End.
Start: Little Hadham crossroads.
Grid reference: TL 440228.
Distance: 7¾ miles (12.5 km).
Ordnance Survey maps: 1:50,000 sheet 167; 1:25,000 sheets TL 41 and TL 42.

This walk is a delightful ramble that for much of the way is made even more pleasant by the proximity of tiny brooks and streams.

Little Hadham, as its name implies, is much smaller than Much Hadham, which we shall visit later on; it is basically an attractive collection of old cottages that was formed around the old windmill. The large building that faces squarely up the hill towards Puckeridge was the Angel Inn. The hamlet seems to have lost some of its character as a result of the conversion of this ancient hostelry to a private house.

The walk starts from the Little Hadham crossroads, at the traffic lights. (You can park along the lane to Albury.) Walk up the hill towards Bishop's Stortford, past the filling station, and turn right by the boundary of the primary school buildings just beyond. The path leads to a field, and skirts it to the right. Climb gently uphill beside the remains of a once elaborate hedge system on your right. Soon to the right there comes a surprise view over to Hadham Ford, while the loss of hedgerows now allows you views also towards Stortford. When you meet a track, go downhill with it as it skirts around a copse and turns left on the lower meadows to pass through a gate ahead. Now you will see the white-painted wooden rails of a footbridge near the houses. Cross this to the road near the iron village pump, a survivor from 1880.

On the far side of the road, go leftwards following the front sweep of the cottages; soon you are on a path that ventures along beside the stream. In about 500 yards you strike another footbridge; cross it to the road again, then go right for about the same distance. After passing a farm, leave the road as it swings away to the right to cross a bridge, and cross a bar-stile by a field-gate on the left so that you continue your direction over the soft grass. The track now runs to the left side of the stream, climbing away from the water. After passing through a field-gate opening, leave the track and aim slightly to the right to go over a stile set in the far right corner of the field. Keep beside a hedge (right), soon passing through a thicker bank of bushes, and continue along a broader track that runs forward along the left side of fields to reach a road. Cross the stile opposite and press forward over grass; you are on the outskirts of Much Hadham, and you can glimpse several ancient buildings through the trees on the right.

The path narrows and winds upwards through a thicket of young trees; here the official footpath should allow you to keep close to the stream, but you will often find it easier to follow the actual path between the trees until you strike a clear track running downhill again. This leads to another footbridge and a very pretty glimpse of Much Hadham church, amongst the finest in Hertfordshire.

Much Hadham. The church of St Andrew dates from the thirteenth century; try and find time for a visit, and note, especially, the great wooden lock. The long village street, with many fine houses, can be reached by continuing ahead.

The walk continues with a left turn at the church to pass a pretty huddle of thatched buildings; this small lane will take you on near the stream. Avoid another tempting footbridge and footpath sign on the left, but go over the stile on the left side as the lane bends sharply to the right. Swing half-leftwards towards another footbridge, and on the far side bear right to follow the left-hand hedge to an iron cage-wicket at a drive that can be seen to divide a few yards uphill. At the side of the right-hand drive is a stile; cross and continue over grass towards another stile that you can glimpse on higher ground. The path roughly follows the line of the drive, then beyond the stile runs close to the hedgeline (with the house beyond) to a stile at a gravelled track. Now move a few yards to the left, and continue on the far side by a path on the right that squeezes between the wire fence ahead and the line of a hedge. Emerging soon into open country, with a hedgeline left, continue to a rural lane, turning left along it to reach a road at a bridge (Dane Bridge).

You now follow the stream for well over a mile by a path that starts on the far side of the bridge, by the red-brick wall of a house. The track strides confidently forward until it reaches a gate, but you simply continue over the grass, following the stream. At a flat bridge, which seems to serve no purpose, you may move a few yards to the left, but continue to follow the electricity poles, with the stream away to your left until, finally, the waters swirl to the right, forcing the path through a gate in the far right end of the long meadow. At once, your path turns to continue its direction beside the stream; do not be lured over another concrete bridge by a tempting track later, but persevere, keeping the path that hugs the right bank of the stream, and you

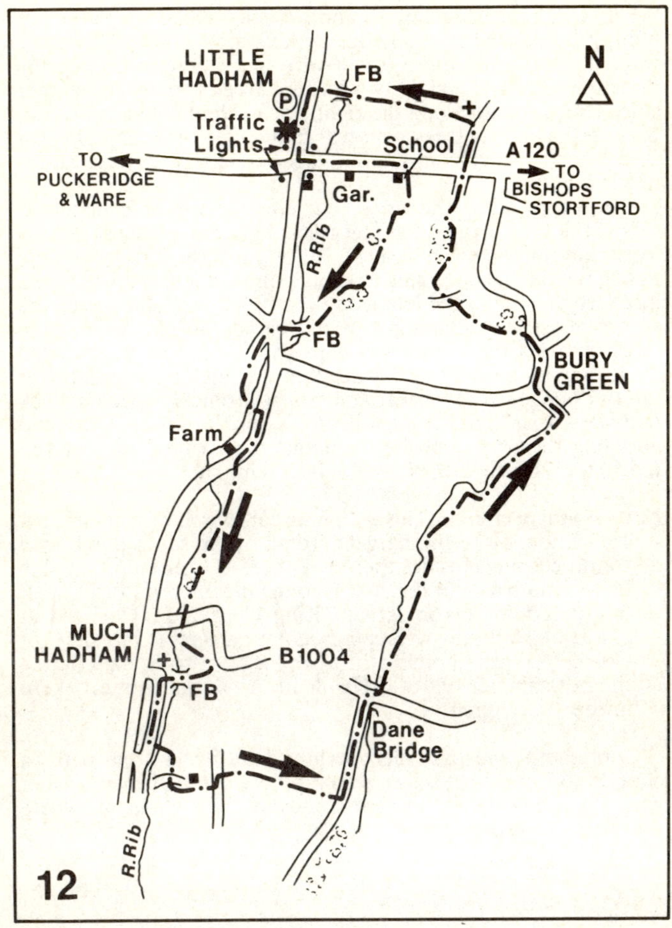

will emerge at a lane, with the houses of Bury Green just to the left.

Walk up to the village green, and bear right with the road, passing the village pond.

Keep left at a road junction about 200 yards ahead, but look for a signposted footpath on the left, some 50 yards from the junction (it also has a tiny bridge). Cross the stile here, and keep beside the right hedgeline to another stile above. In the upper field, gradually leave the hedge by keeping forward. When the walk was surveyed there was a wire fence here indicating the direction. Soon you pass two ancient trees and reach another stile. Cross and go along the right side of the field ahead. After passing the side of trees, you will find a stile on your right that admits you to a wide and rather vague trackway. A little care is needed here.

Do not go along the track, but cross to the field opposite; follow the line of the ditch that runs along the left side (avoid a track that runs between bushes). In 150 yards, bear right with the line of the ditch, continuing to keep it on your left. You will see a large wood over to the left, and you will also be able to see the church at Little Hadham in normal weather. Just keep along the sides of fields until your way clips the far end of the wooded area, then swing right again, keeping the ditch on your left (for the old hedges have gone), and you will quickly strike a track that leads at once to the main Bishop's Stortford road. Cross and go along the lane opposite, turning left at a farm so that you reach the churchyard of St Cecilia's church.

Little Hadham church. This is an unusual church with an unusual dedication. Note the bargeboarding of the south porch with trefoil cusping. Inside, there is a three-decker pulpit. A slab on the south side of the altar is to the memory of Lord Capel, 'murdered for his loyalty to King Charles I'. He lived at Hadham Hall and was captured by Fairfax at the siege of Colchester, after holding the town for seventy-six days during the hot summer of 1648. His death mask was formerly kept inside the church.

Continue ahead past the porch and on by the fine path (a churchway), which reaches a final footbridge and then a lane, where you bear left to the crossroads at Little Hadham, where the walk started.

13. Buntingford

Circular walk from Buntingford by way of Aspenden, Westmill and Owles Estate.
Start: Buntingford High Street, Baldock road.
Grid reference: TL 363294.
Distance: 6 miles (9.7 km).
Ordnance Survey maps: 1:50,000 sheet 166; 1:25,000 sheet TL 32.

This is a short walk around the old town of Buntingford, which stands astride the main coaching road to Cambridge and so is a place of ancient inns, wooden beams and wonderful old houses. The villages nearby, which we will visit, are amongst the most picturesque in Hertfordshire and no photographer's album is complete without a view of the ancient canopied pump and village green at Westmill.

Buntingford. Like most places in Hertfordshire, this town has its sprawl of new houses, but the main street remains a place of history, filled with houses, shops and inns, some dating from Georgian times. The railway from St Margarets, a wonderful single-track branch that served a number of halts lit by oil lamps, was closed in 1964. While the hopes of the Victorian promoters of the railway for the growth of the town failed to be realised, an immense modern development by Sainsbury's has at last forced the expansion of Buntingford. The Sainsbury's sprawl will be viewed during the walk.

Leave Buntingford by the main Baldock road (A507). After 300 yards, pass Monks Way on your left; some 100 yards beyond this turning, as the road starts a slight right curve, turn left on a gravelled drive lined with a row of cottages (signposted). Continue past a small factory, and follow the path through an alley to emerge at another estate road. Cross directly and follow up to a stile on a rising field. The path strikes over the field, half-left, giving fine open views to your left. Cross a stile in the far hedge and, following a wire fence on your right, keep forward with the grassy path, which drops downhill to an unexpected little wooden footbridge set amid the trees at the bottom of the field. From the stile on the far side, strike slightly left over grass, aiming for the centre of the treeline on the left. The derelict mansion away on the right is Aspenden Hall, where Lord Macaulay, the historian, attended the school held by the Reverend Matthew Preston. From the stile in the trees, a few yards will take you to the leafy churchyard of St Mary's, Aspenden. At the village street go left to the green.

Aspenden. The church, with thirteenth-century lancets, was restored by Blomfield in 1873. Inside is the tomb of Sir Robert Clifford, lord of the manor, who secured his position and power by betraying his fellow conspirators in the Perkin Warbeck affair in the 1480s. It is still a village of considerable wealth, as can be glimpsed from walking down towards the village green. In April 1924 there was considerable national interest in the mysterious disappearance of Mrs Brightling, wife of the innkeeper of the old Red Lion in the village, after police started to probe the blackened ruins of the inn, which had been burnt down seven years previously. Her seventy-year-old husband was the subject of village rumours that he had allowed his wife to perish in the flames. Her remains were never discovered.

On reaching the village green, cross to the swings and play area on the right, then bear right to cross a footbridge to the lane, where you turn left towards Westmill. There is no footpath for the three quarters of a mile to Westmill village, but the quiet lane provides some fine views. At Westmill, bear left at the green (and pump), passing the church and public house (the Bird in Hand).

Westmill. Often said to be the most photographed village in Hertfordshire, Westmill was the home of the historian Cussans, who wrote a readable account of the *History of Hertfordshire* in 1728. The church has Anglo-Saxon origins but is the work of many ages.

At a road fork a short distance beyond the church, bear left to cross the river and carry on up to the main road. There is no alternative for the 400 yard walk to the left along the main road, but cross to the opposite side and use the footpath. Near the foot of the small valley you will find a broad track on the right, clearly signposted. It runs beside a line of trees. Leave the main road now and follow the track, keeping the hedgeline on your left as you slowly make your way on to higher ground. The path bends left with the hedgeline, then right as it approaches a small wood (Camp Wood), which can be clearly seen on the high ground. At the trees, climb up a small bank on your left, and continue to follow the side of fields, making sure that you pass the wood on your *right* hand. Over to the left you will see the Sainsbury depot.

The hedgeside path soon breaks out into an open drive at the farm approach to Owles; take the broad track that runs ahead in the direction you have been travelling. You will pass Owles Hall soon on your right. The rutted drive will then take you past another wonderful old farm, Alswick Hall. Soon you pass a pond

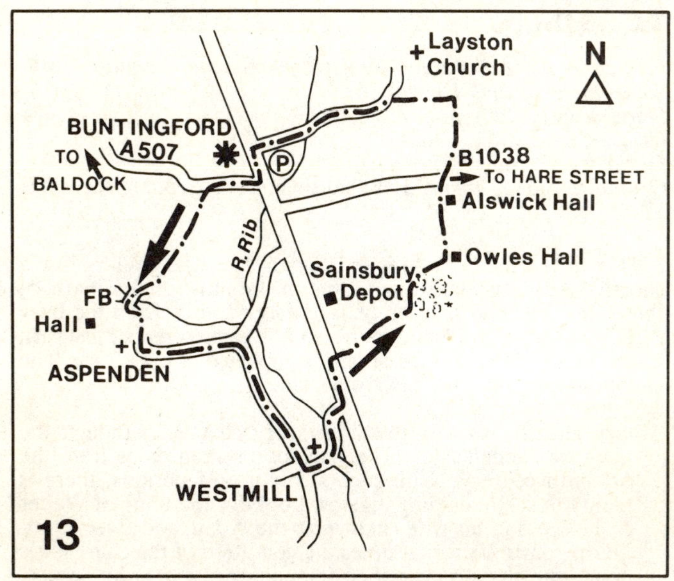

and reach a road. Cross directly to the track opposite and when, after 300 yards, it meets a crossing track go left along it, in line with the electricity poles, and keep forward until you reach a narrow strip of grass leading almost at once to a small lane. It is worth turning right to visit the church which you can clearly see.

Layston, where we now are, was the earliest settlement in the Buntingford area and is Anglo-Saxon in origin. The church, now a romantic ruin apart from its well secured chancel, was the focus of this little community, but the coach route in the valley drew local people down the hill, and it became increasingly difficult for local people to make the half-mile trip back to Layston church. It is now one of the quietest spots in Hertfordshire, although the final damage to the church occurred only during the Second World War.

After visiting the church, turn back along the road and go downhill to reach Buntingford by the small brick bridge over the river. As you go, note the small brick building, little bigger than a shed, near the bridge. It was the village lock-up, and tradition has it that the inmates were refreshed during their incarceration by means of a teapot spout inserted through a hole in the door.

14. Albury

Circular walk from Albury by way of Southend, Patmore Heath nature reserve and Upwick Wood
Start: Albury church.
Grid reference: TL 436248.
Distance: 3½ miles (5.6 km).
Ordnance Survey maps: 1:50,000 sheet 167; 1:25,000 sheet TL 42.

This little ramble is designed for anyone who prefers just a short walk; it passes through some of the most remote parts of the county. Albury is a tiny village about a mile from the busy A120 road to Bishop's Stortford, so it is easy to reach: just turn up the lane at Hadham crossroads, signposted to the village. The church is on the rise, on a side lane.

Albury church has a thirteenth-century chancel, although the nave was added later. The fine rood screen dates from the fifteenth century. With such a mixture of periods, there is plenty to see, including brasses. Look for the tomb of Walter de la Lee and his wife (known as the Adam and Eve tomb). During early Victorian times the condition of the church was poor, and the curate bribed the congregation to be absent.

Start the walk from an iron kissing gate that can be found at the rear of the churchyard, just left of an elaborate tomb guarded by complex wrought ironwork. The path goes straight forward from the gate under an avenue of limes and continues beside a hedge to run down to a valley, with splendid views. You may find a lone way-marker in the dip. Carry straight on, beside the trees on your left, to reach a broad crossing track. Go straight on, now with a wood on your right. Keep the hedge on your right, as the border path soon has fields on each side, and, 600 yards after crossing the track and immediately after passing another wood on the right, turn right along the path that runs beside the other face of the wood, so that the trees remain on the right. The way leads over a concrete river bridge and up to a lane at Southend, which you pass by making a right turn along the lane.

Soon, in 200 yards, the fine old thatched inn, the Catherine Wheel, appears on the left; here turn up the tiny lane on the left for another 200 yards, taking the first lane on the right, leading to the Patmore Heath nature reserve, the area of scrub and woodland on your left. An attractive array of individually styled houses on the right-hand side looks out over the valley.

Note the pond with its sedges and water irises as the lane

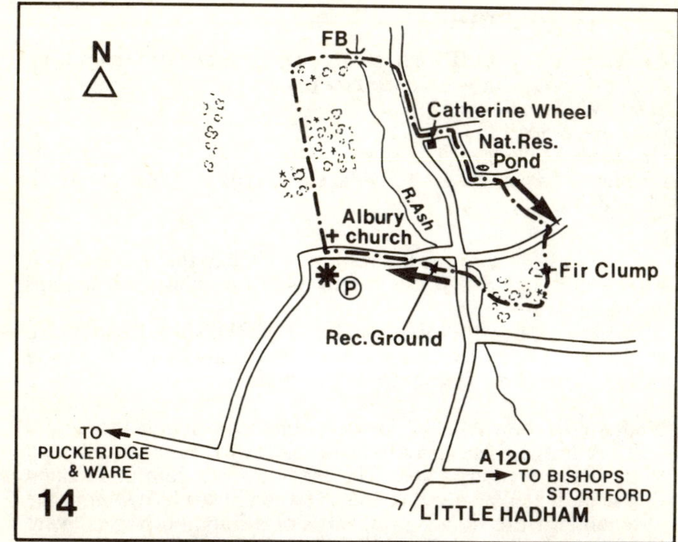

makes a sharp bend to the left. Soon start to look out for a signposted track on the right, some 180 yards beyond the bend, and at the start of a brick boundary wall. Go down this as it wanders across a valley and up to a metalled lane by a remote thatched cottage.

Now take care; the way is by a right turn for a few yards along the lane (passing a pond in the bushes on the left); then take the second of two broad field tracks that start, almost together, on the left. With a dip and the remains of a once fine hedgerow (now chopped down) on your left, climb up to pass a stand of firs in the distance. After the track runs past these trees (on the right), you now reach a small area of open farmland in a dip before passing the next wood, also on your right hand.

When the track runs clear of the wood, take a broad crossing path, after some 100 yards, running down the length of the field to the right, so that you go towards another part of the wood in the distance. This is Upwick Wood, and the path soon wanders delightfully downhill through the trees until you reach open meadowland at the foot. Keep generally forward in the direction you have been taking, and reach a lane by a small bridge. Now go right but turn in left by a footpath some 100 yards away on the opposite side of the road. You pass allotments and a recreation ground to strike a lane, which runs uphill towards your starting point of Albury church.

15. Wadesmill

Circular walk from Wadesmill by way of Standon Green End, Collier's End, Barwick and Youngsbury.
Start: Wadesmill village.
Grid reference: TL 359175.
Distance: 7½ miles (12.1 km).
Ordnance Survey maps: 1:50,000 sheet 166; 1:25,000 sheets TL 31 and TL 32.

This is a walk through the rolling country of the Rib valley. It has everything — views, woods and the plash of streams tumbling over fords.

The walk starts from Wadesmill on the Old North Road, north of Ware. Parking can be found off the main road in the old village across the bridge from the main inns.

Wadesmill. The village has moved from its ancient centre at old Thundridge church to the main road, where the Anchor and the Feathers inns stand. The first turnpike gate in England was built at Wadesmill in 1663. It was a busy place; before the coming of the railways 'upwards of a hundred horses' were often stabled at the Feathers. There is an obelisk, halfway up the hill towards Puckeridge, in memory of Thomas Clarkson, who at that spot resolved to devote his life to the movement to abolish the slave trade.

Walk past the Anchor and the Feathers along the main road towards Puckeridge, keeping on the opposite side to the Feathers. Beyond the cottages on the left and a small modern development, the road starts to climb; turn off left at the small blind lane here; you pass a house called Athena and approach a drive with a large shed on the left in a few yards. The footpath starts at a point between the shed (left) and a large iron driveway post; you will find that you simply have to walk forward with a steep ditch on the left and gardens on your right for 50 yards or so to cross a clear iron footbridge to the far side of the depression which marks a dried-up river course of the Bourne. Now on the left bank, the path runs clearly ahead, at first near the lower slopes but soon climbing until you are walking ahead on the right side of a vast field, with the bushes marking the very steep depression of the stream on your right hand.

Carry on for 300 yards, after which the path drops to cross a footbridge before continuing, still by the side of the open farmland, for another quarter of a mile to reach a small lane twisting up from High Cross. Continue by the path directly opposite, simply keeping the depression on your right.

After walking for another half mile you should be able to

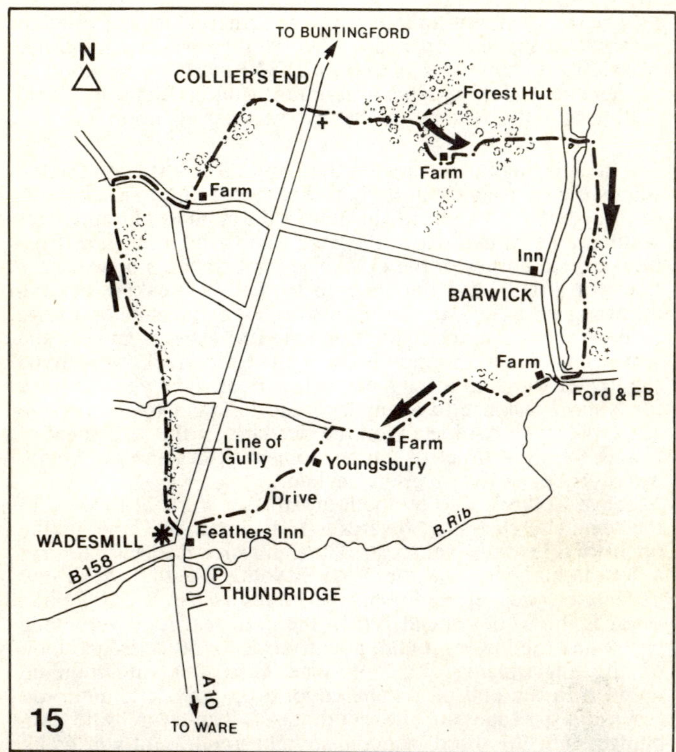

glimpse the roofs of isolated buildings in the distance. Near here, also, the depression and its attendant bushes make a sharp right turn away as a bold wide track strikes forward uphill towards a cottage. Keep your direction by following this track over the field to the cottage, where you will find a small lane forming a sharp bend. Go right now, following the lane across a valley; at the top of the next rise you reach a large house on the right, and a lane turning. The few houses near this junction form the hamlet of Standon Green End.

Standon Green End entered the history books in 1784. Elizabeth Brett, a farm maid working in the brewhouse of a nearby farm, was startled to see an immense red and white object floating in the air towards her. It was the first flight of a hydrogen balloon in England bumping to earth, having left the Artillery Ground at Moorfields, London, earlier that day.

> The occupant was an Italian named Lunardi, accompanied by a cat, a pigeon and a dog. The landing was accomplished safely. A stone was placed in a field marking the point of descent and a suitable inscription noting Lunardi's flight through 'the legions of the air' was placed upon it.

After passing the turning on the right, cross a stile on the left side of the road almost at once, to a path that runs to the left side of a large farm. Keep to the right side of the field and cross another stile, which is set in a small wood, about 50 yards from the far right corner of the field. The path wanders between the trees for a delightful 100 yards or so, before breaking out and following on a track that runs forward along the side of a large field, with trees on the right. There are fine views from here and also from higher ground reached after the track has curved slightly leftwards to reach a hedgeline. Bear right with the track for a short distance to a tiny lane and follow it to the right to reach the main road again on the outskirts of the settlement of Collier's End — a petrol station, some cottages and the Lamb, where good food can often be had.

Leave Collier's End by the footpath that starts at the side of the small church, some 80 yards left of your arrival lane, on the opposite side of the main road. The signposted bridleway follows a left-hand hedge all the way; beyond the first field, the hedgeline winds left and then right to follow the line of a ditch towards the woods ahead. When the path reaches a very deep brook and the lower ground, go leftwards for 50 yards and look for the single planks of a footbridge. Cross this, and continue uphill with the end of a small coppice on your left, until you reach the dark mass of the wood ahead. The clear, wide path plunges into the wood, running straight uphill until you break out into a large forest clearing with a small dilapidated brick lodge ahead. Immediately after passing this retreat, you will be presented with a choice of forest tracks. Ignore the one directly ahead, and take the track that runs off half-right. The track is quite clear and will bring you up, through Plashes Wood, in 300 yards to open ground near a lonely farm. After passing one side of the property, turn left along a crossing track for 60 yards or so before going right again by a grassy field track that passes to the right side of a large pond.

With the house behind you, continue towards the far hedge and the two clear oaks ahead. On reaching the hedge, the original line of the way seems to be lost and by turning leftwards at this point and following the hedgeline on your right you soon reach a clear footpath that runs forward from the corner of the wood ahead. The path runs just inside the edge of the wood for a time, dropping so that it passes later between the trees on either side. This idyllic woodland way then breaks out to run ahead along the side of the field to a collection of cottages at Latchford.

Go left for 10 or 15 yards, then downhill by a lane to cross the river by a footbridge at a ford. Some 60 yards beyond, on the far side, a signpost marks a bridleway starting from a gate on the right. This becomes another pretty path that runs along level ground, with trees left, and the river on the right below.

When the path arrives at a gate, open it and continue ahead through ground that becomes increasingly dotted with bushes and scrub. Later the path is lined on either side with bushes, then runs on as a track until you drop steeply to a lane at Barwick Ford.

Beyond the footbridge on the right bear left on a signposted trackway that leads past farm buildings before turning leftwards out of the valley. This good track runs on for a straight 300 yards before turning squarely right (signposted) to follow the line of a ditch. Soon it turns again, this time leftwards, and breasts the rise to give fine views, behind, over Barwick. Simply keep on the farm track as it passes the side of woods until, in half a mile, it reaches the approach to Home Farm, Youngsbury. Here bear to the right along the clear cross track before the farm buildings and when, in 400 yards, it reaches another drive entering from the left, turn off along this wide track. Soon you will pass a house and then a stable block and shortly glimpse the facade of Youngsbury House.

Youngsbury. The house dates partly from 1745, with large nineteenth-century additions. The park, through which you are now walking, was designed and laid out by 'Capability' Brown, although during the 1920s and 1930s a vast number of trees were felled to satisfy the London market in logs for domestic burning.

Continue along the drive into the valley and when, near Wadesmill village, you come to a fork, bear right. You will pass a short row of modern houses and reach the main road again beside the Feathers inn.

Index